ILLUSTRATED TALES OF COUNTY DURHAM

STUART MILLER

AMBERLEY

First published 2026

Amberley Publishing
The Hill, Stroud
Gloucestershire, GL5 4EP

www.amberley-books.com

British Library Cataloguing in Publication Data.
A catalogue record for this book is available from the British Library.

ISBN 978 1 3981 2993 1 (paperback)
ISBN 978 1 3981 2994 8 (ebook)

Origination by Amberley Publishing.
Printed in Great Britain.

Appointed GPSR EU Representative:
Easy Access System Europe Oü, 16879218
Address: Mustamäe tee 50, 10621, Tallinn, Estonia
Contact Details: gpsr.requests@easproject.com, +358 40 500 3575

Contents

Introduction: Where to Begin?

The County Durham I write about is the one that existed before 1972 legislation removed South Tyneside, Sunderland, Gateshead, Hartlepool and Stockton-on-Tees and added fragments of North Yorkshire. In 1996, Stockton and Hartlepool were returned but Sunderland, Gateshead and South Tyneside remain part of Tyne and Wear. However, all are happily reunited here!

As for folk tales, they are, I think, generally understood to be stories that have been orally transmitted between generations over many years. They are inclusive since they tend to identify people as part of a group, national or regional, but they are also potentially exclusive because they may not resonate with people outside those groups. Folk tales are by no means invented from scratch. Many are based upon some sort of initial factual essence. Fact and folk tale can become inextricably entwined and often be made more colourful by the addition of real names and places.

On with the stories then, and the obvious place to begin is with dragons.

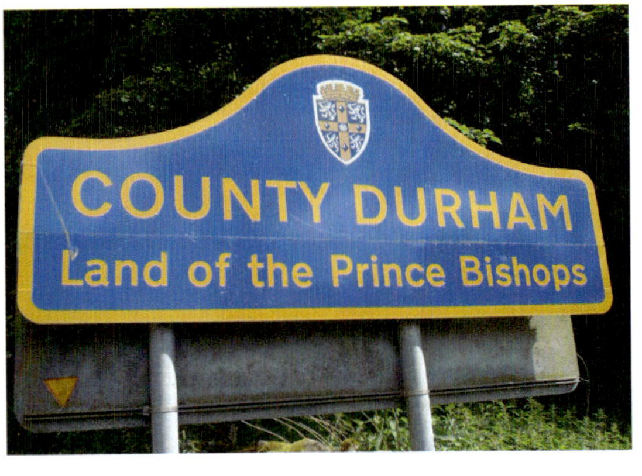

County Durham was part of the county palatine governed by the bishop with vice regal authority. The palatine rights were abolished in 1836 but the 'Land of the Prince Bishops' endures as an eye-catching road sign.

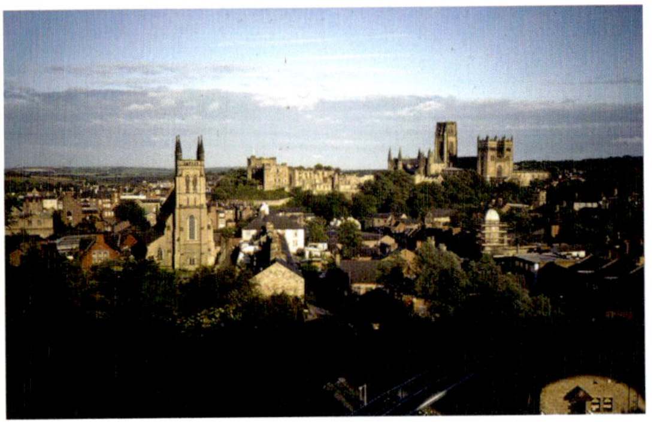

Durham is the county town of County Durham. County Durham is the only English county normally referred to with the prefix, which helps to distinguish between the county and the city.

I

Here Be Dragons

There are other dragon tales in the wider region, but familiarity with the Lambton Worm is almost a defining feature of County Durham natives. And this dragon story has everything a dragon story should have.

Young John Lambton, heir to the estate, was a rebellious boy. He scorned his tutors and defied his old father. He delighted in breaking rules laid down for his guidance. Above all, on Sundays he would miss church and go off to fish. One Sunday he was idly casting his line into the River Wear as local folk passed by and complained about the behaviour of their future lord. He sat for hours without even seeing a fish. Again and again he cast his line. Again and again it came up empty. Then at last he felt a catch. Indeed, he thought he had caught a fine salmon so much did it struggle. However, what he landed was an evil-looking creature, half newt and half eel, which wriggled and wrapped itself around his line. Furiously Lambton tore it loose and hurled it down a well. He gave no more thought to it for many years and went off to learn the skills and duties of a knight. When he reached manhood he went off to fight in the Crusades.

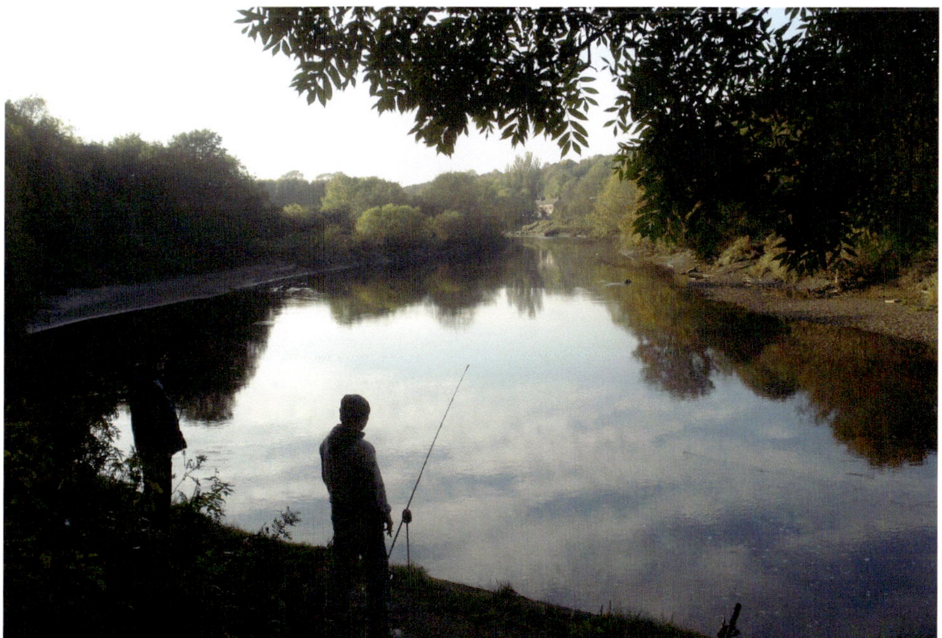

Fishermen missing church near Biddick on a November Sunday, just as young John Lambton must have been doing when overtaken by fate.

Meanwhile the worm grew and grew until it could coil itself three times around Penshaw Hill. It began to venture into the surrounding countryside in search of food. It devoured sheep and lambs, and sucked the cows dry. It rampaged across cornfields and devastated the crops. The old Lord of Lambton was driven to his wits' end by the damage caused by the beast. So notorious had it become that knights journeyed from far afield to gain glory by killing the monster. All came to grief because not only did it have fiery breath and enormous claws it had the amazing ability to regenerate body parts. So for seven long, awful years it enjoyed untrammelled access to the lands along the river's sides.

Then one day the son of Lambton returned. By now he was a man of great courage and martial skill. When he heard of the trouble inflicted upon the Lambton estate he swore he would end it – as he had been the cause of it so many years before. However, before he went, he sought an answer to the magical powers it possessed. He turned to a wise old witch who lived nearby. Her advice was sound. She told him to confront the worm on its favourite rock in the middle of the Wear and to let it attack him there. He was, she said, to have a suit of armour, studded with blades, made for himself. As the beast attempted to crush him in its coils, it would cut itself to pieces which would then wash away down the river.

Thankful for this help, the young knight asked what price she required. Her answer was chilling: 'When you have killed the worm and return home you must

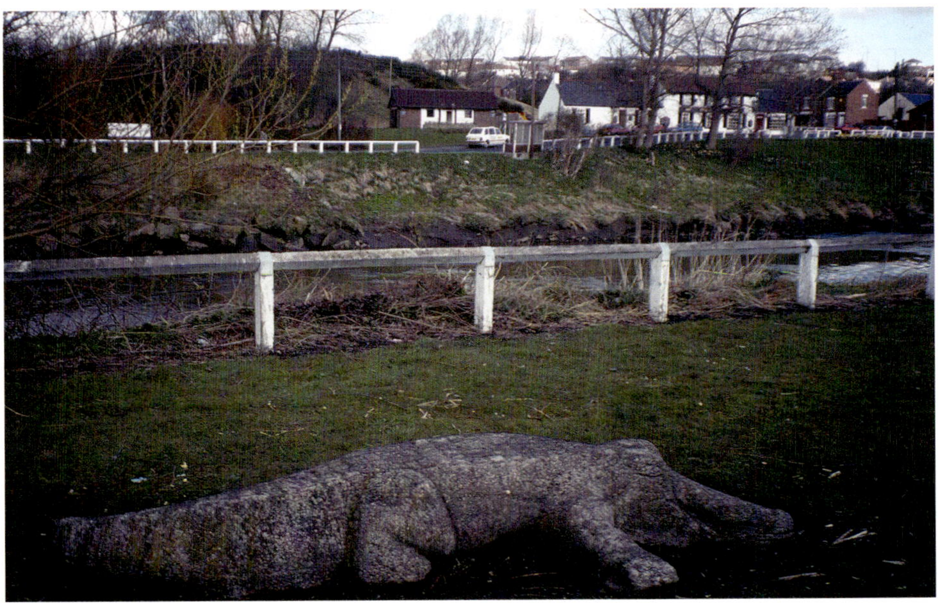

The sculptor of the concrete crocodile at Penshaw was Stanley Bonnar. Crocodiles are one of the many inspirations for dragon stories, although dragons are usually represented as being composites of several creatures. The smooth, rounded Worm Hill in the background was one of the resting places for the Lambton Worm.

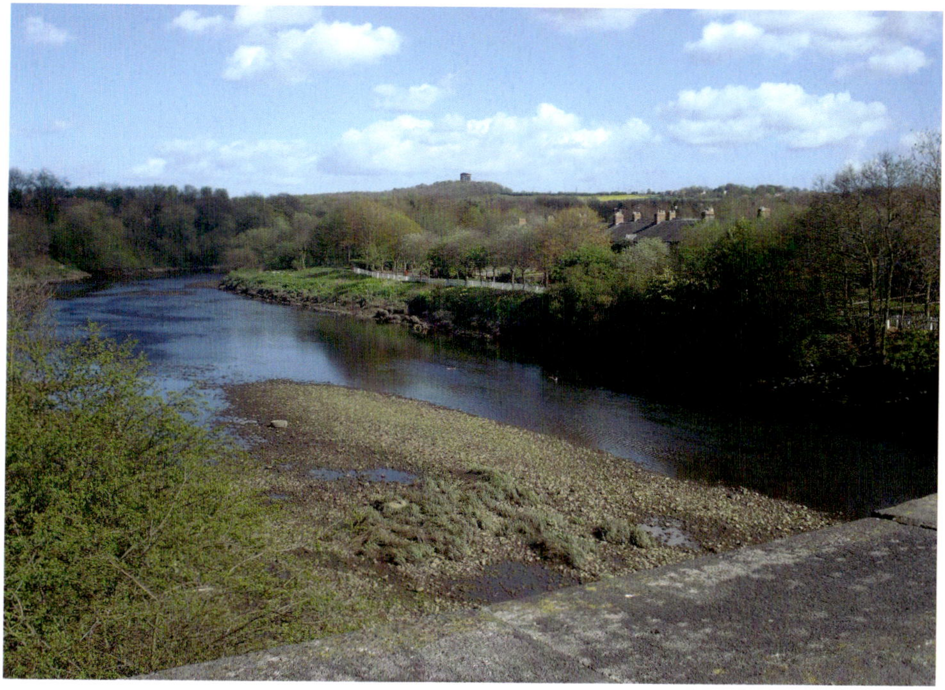

The view downstream from Biddick Bridge. This was the area patrolled by the Lambton Worm. Penshaw Monument is visible in the middle distance.

kill the first living thing you meet. If you fail to do so, the Lords of Lambton for nine generations will never die peacefully in their beds.'

The young knight hurried home to tell his father that he knew how to master the beast. When the worm was dead, he would blow a bugle. Then his father was to let loose one of his old hounds. It would run to greet the young lord and be the first living thing he met.

So, Lambton set off to confront the worm. When it saw him, it bellowed with rage and attempted to seize him. With one blow he sliced away a section of its thrashing tail and the bloody flesh was carried away by the ebbing waters of the Wear. The great beast coiled itself about Lambton's body but the tighter it grasped the deeper the blades cut and the more furious it became. He managed to free his arm and cut off more of its body which, piece by piece, floated down the river. At last he stood victorious on the rock.

Then he made his way back towards the castle. He blew his bugle to signal his victory. To his horror, his father forgot to release the hound, and rushed to embrace him, so his own father was the first living creature he met. He thrust his sword into the hound loping along by his father in the hope that the price would still be paid. It was in vain though. Although there was great rejoicing, the curse of the witch was not lifted. From that day, not one of the Lords of Lambton died in bed for nine generations.

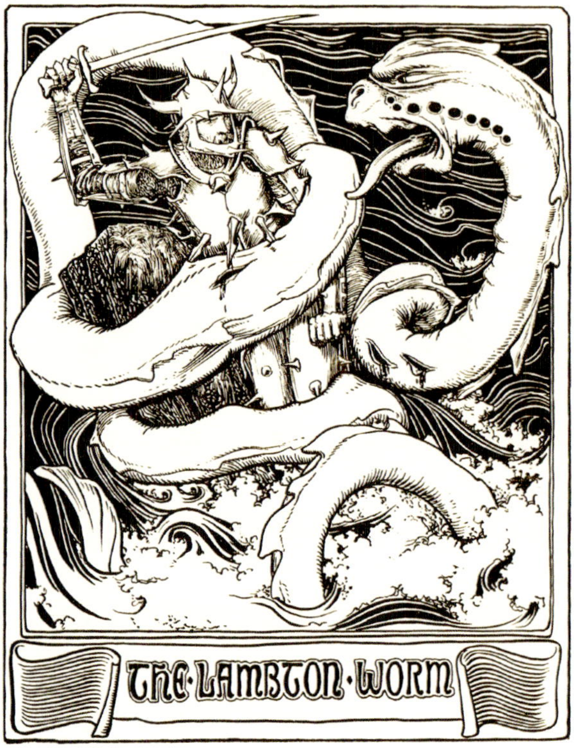

The Lambton Worm from *More English Fairy Tales* by Joseph Jacobs, 1894. Illustration by John D. Batten. This is the classic image of the renowned encounter between brave Sir John and the goggle-eyed monster.

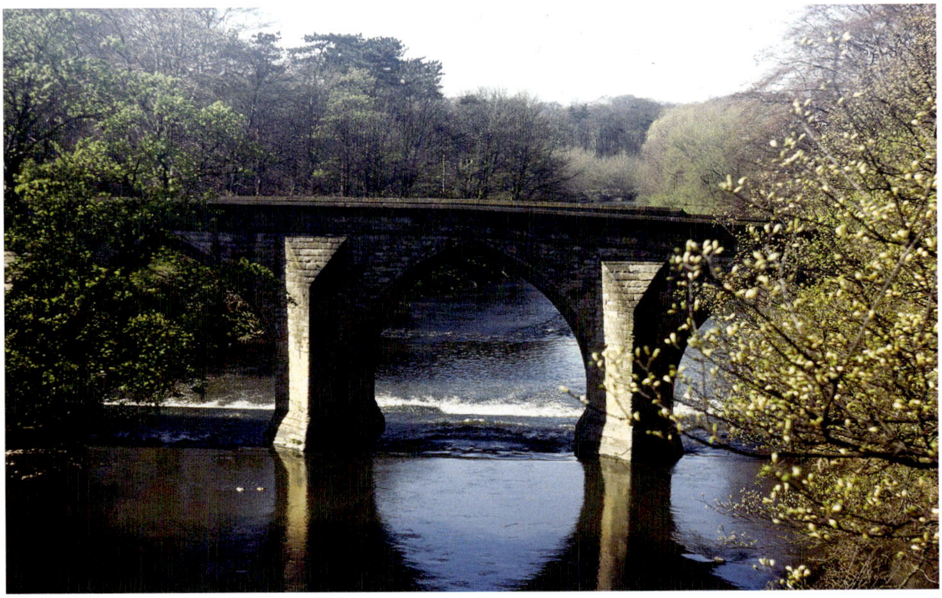

Henry Lambton of the ninth generation did not die on the fifteenth-century New Bridge into the Lambton estate in 1794 as is usually claimed, but in 1761 on the Lamb Bridge inside the estate. The New Bridge is now closed. Taken from the busy A183.

The other great dragon story of County Durham is about the Sockburn Worm. The usual version is as follows.

The people living along the banks of the Tees once lived in great terror of an awful dragon or wyrm. Death, devastation and famine haunted the land and resulted in great sadness and despair. No one knew from whence the creature had come but all knew it lived in a lair near a well in a loop in the river between Yarm and Darlington. There it lurked. In the daytime it sheltered from the rays of the sun. Then when it was hungry, it ventured forth. The local inhabitants built a huge trough and filled it daily with fresh milk. But this was not enough to assuage the needs of the dragon. And when it had drunk the milk, and rested its great body, it would return to attack and destroy as before.

Only Sir John Conyers, Lord of the Manor, could save his land. He dressed himself in his armour and went to the Chapel of All Saints where, in the dark silence, he spent the whole night in vigil. Then he returned to his hall and took up his sword – the Conyers Falchion, a great single-edged sword. At first light, Sir John went forth and waited for the return of the dragon. As the sun rose and the heat grew, the dragon returned. It sought out its lair to lie and rest but what it found was the edge of Sir John's great sword.

A furious battle began as the huge creature endeavoured to grip the knight in its coils. However, his armour was strong and withstood the test. Finally, he

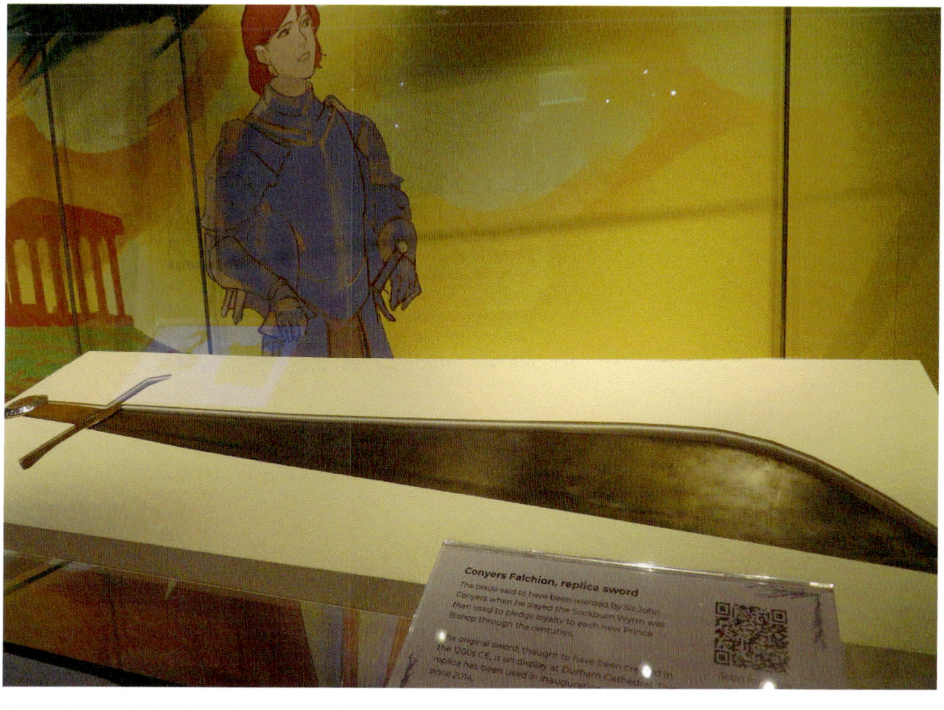

A replica of the Sockburn Falchion in the temporary Beasts and Legends exhibition in Durham University Library in 2025.

managed to bring his sword down with one last swing separating head from neck. Dark blood flooded into silvery waters. The task was done and the people rejoiced at their freeing from the beast. Sir John had them take the huge body and bury it in a great pit. Then they took a great grey slab of limestone and laid it over the top. The king, hearing of this great victory, confirmed the possession of the manor forever by the Lords of Sockburn and their descendants. To mark the deed, he ordered that the Falchion should be presented symbolically to each new Prince Bishop of Durham as he crossed the Tees at Sockburn to enter Durham.

The legend of the Lambton Worm may date from the fourteenth century but is especially memorable because of the famous music hall song written in 1867 by C. M. Leumane. It was the basis of *The Lair of the White Worm*, a horror novel by Bram Stoker, upon which was based a film by Ken Russell. Various landmarks are associated with the story. There is a Worm Hill at Biddick. There was once a significant rock in the middle of the channel which was blasted away in the nineteenth century. Knowledgeable locals point sagely at track marks around Penshaw Hill and tell gullible visitors that they are the marks of the coils of the Lambton Worm.

The Lambton family is an ancient line which may predate the Norman Conquest. Many did die violent deaths. But then they would, because they were frequently serving as soldiers. The last of the nine generations, Henry Lambton,

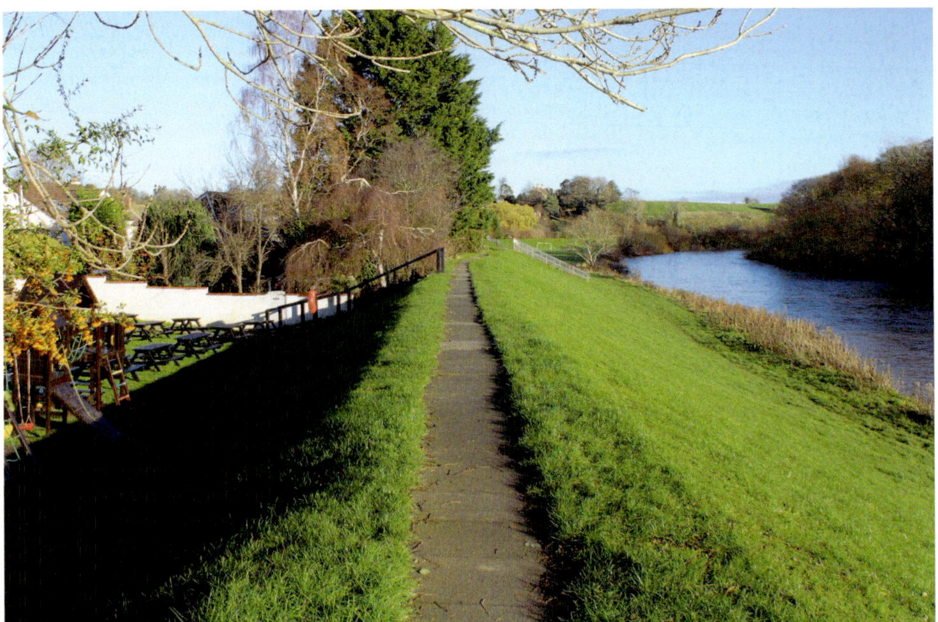

Originally the strange ritual of swapping the Sockburn Falchion happened at Neasham Ford near the Fox and Hounds Inn. This was the nearest crossing point to Sockburn, but the course of the Tees changed and the ford is now gone. So, the exchange moved to Croft Bridge and then to Elvet Bridge.

allegedly, died in his carriage of a heart attack while crossing the Chester New Bridge on 26 June 1761. Hopeful children still fish along the banks. The curious story about the old hound and the father is in the same category as that of the death of Aegeus, the father of Theseus. The story is, of course, moralistic. Lambton brought this all about because of his impiety. It may be that it is a sort of tongue-in-cheek justification for the Lambton ownership of their extensive lands, preferable to the reality that knights were often no more than armed thugs holding their estates by the sword.

As far as the Sockburn Worm is concerned, the Conyers Falchion is one of the great treasures of Durham Cathedral. It is beautifully decorated with engravings of grotesque creatures on the guard. It has been suggested that the sword was produced and engraved to celebrate the deed rather than being the weapon with which the deed was performed. It has been dated *c.* 1260–70. The Blacketts who inherited it attached a label to it with 1063 as the date when the dragon was killed. That would be impossible if the sword was produced 200 years later – unless it was a copy of an original.

The ancient Chapel of All Saints was reduced to a ruin because the Blacketts wanted a romantic Gothic feature to gaze upon. It is claimed that the effigy of a knight is that of Sir John. A hogback Viking gravestone is embellished with an image of the battle between Tyr the Norse god and the giant wolf Fenyr. The tale is claimed to be the inspiration for Lewis Carroll's *Jabberwocky* which he wrote while in Croft and Whitburn. Sockburn was also the romantic setting for

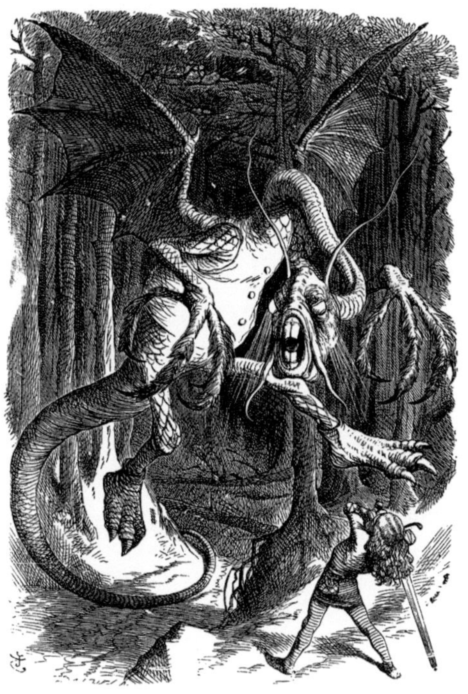

The Jabberwocky, as illustrated by John Tenniel in 1871, is said to have been inspired by the Sockburn Worm. Charles Lutwidge Dodgson, better known as Lewis Carroll, had a very close connection with the area. His father was the rector at Croft-on-Tees.

the meeting of William Wordsworth with his future wife Mary Hutchinson. The Greystone survives albeit cracked. Greystones appear elsewhere in legends. In Beowulf the hero fights the dragon at the 'harne stan' and Tolkien has a greystone at the entrance to Smaug's treasure. As far as the well is concerned, this may be related to the sulphur wells at Dinsdale Spa near Middleton-One-Row which became famous as a watering resort.

According to different versions, the exchange should take place at Sockburn or Neasham Ford or at Croft. In 1661 there is a reference to the 'usual ceremony' when Bishop John Cosin crossed the Tees. This was associated with a recitation of the deed for which the sword had been used. In fact, the ceremony may date from 1386. In recent times the old tradition has been revived, but with the handover on the Elvet Bridge. The Conyers line ended in 1810. By then their lands had been taken over by the Blacketts from Newcastle. If you are wondering who exchanges the sword with incoming bishops nowadays, it is the Mayor of Darlington.

If you enjoy a rollicking good dragon story you will also love stories about wild boars or brawns.

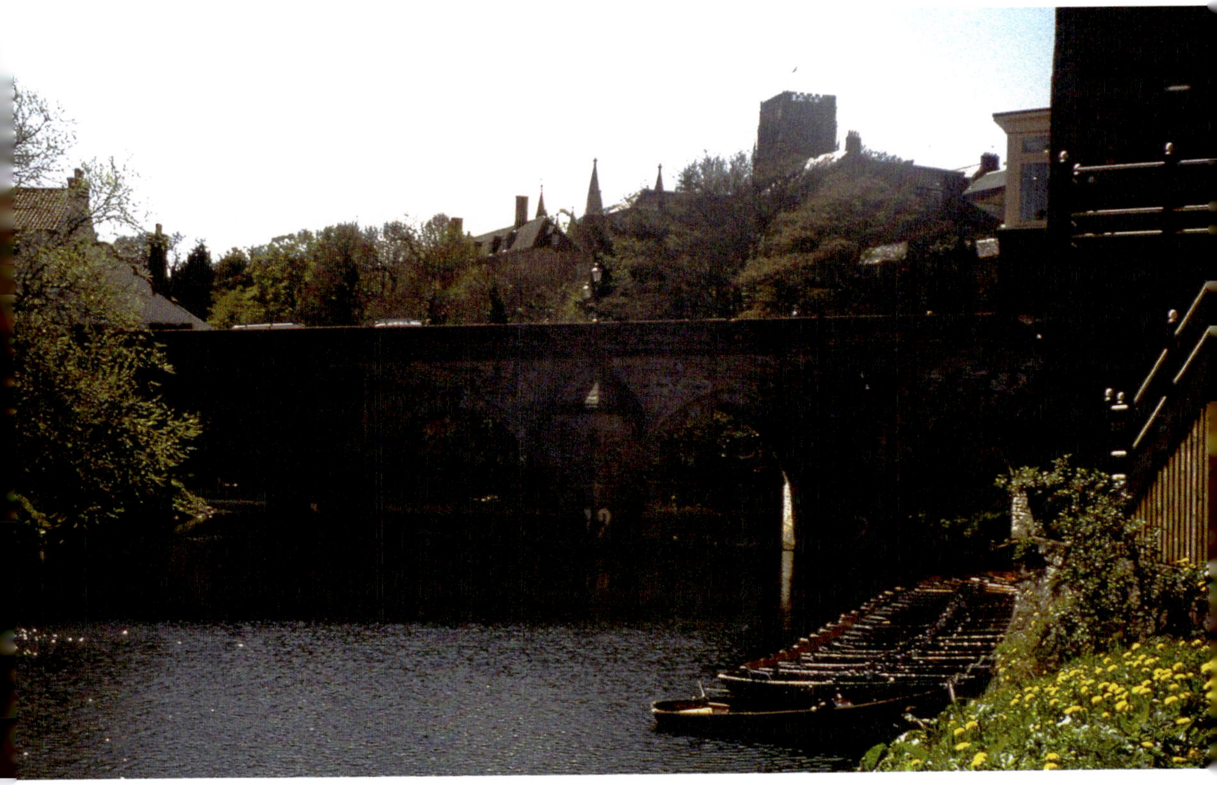

The medieval Elvet Bridge in Durham was built in 1170. The curious falchion ceremony was revived in 1973, and Elvet Bridge is now the venue. The original venue was Neasham Ford (near the welcoming Fox and Hounds) and then, when the Tees changed course, the medieval bridge at Croft-on-Tees.

2

Brains and Brawn

Dragons are exceptionally daunting but they aren't real, which can't be said for wild boars.

The fearsome Brawn of Brancepeth was an enormous boar which fed mostly on roots and acorns, but villagers were afraid to go out alone or let their children play out of their sight because it was very aggressive. According to Surtees, referring to an Old English poem from the very early thirteenth century, it was:

> A formidable toothy boar, which made his lair on Brandon-hill, and walked the forest in ancient undisputed sovereignty from the Wear to the Gaunless. The marshy, and then woody vale, extending from Croxdale to Ferry-wood, was one of the brawn's favourite haunts, affording roots and mast, and the luxurious pleasure of volulation.

According to Brockie, it was an enterprising young man called Hodge, or Roger, who realised that the boar always followed a straight line from Ferryhill to the

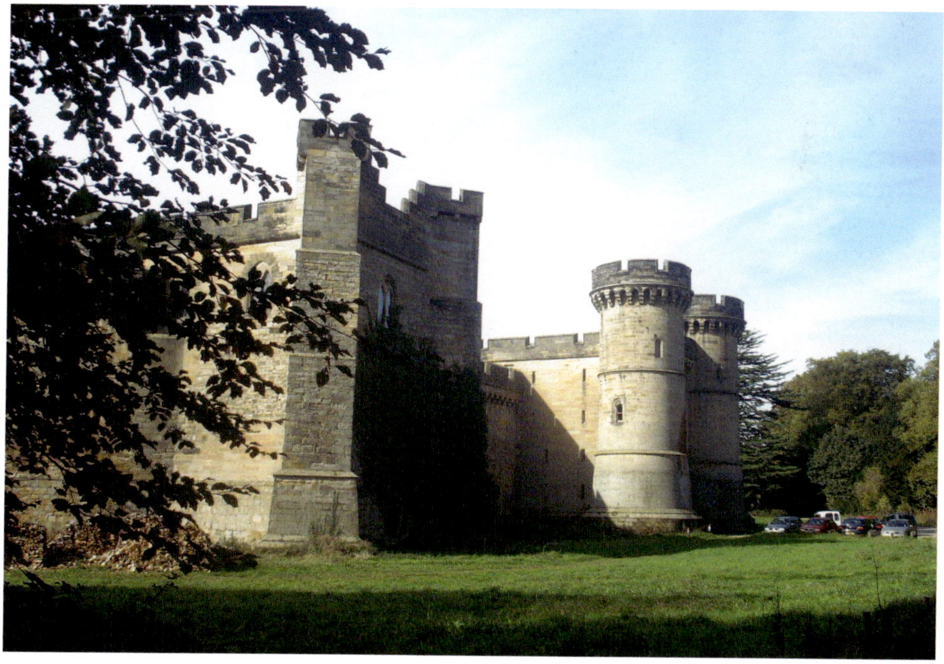

Brancepeth Castle was the site of a Norman fortress but it was heavily reconstructed in the nineteenth century by the wealthy Russells, who made their money from exporting coal.

woods at Mainsforth, so he dug a pit which he covered with turf. Then he lured the brawn towards it. It fell through the covering, and he plunged his spear into its side. Job done!

The story is always included in any respectable compendium of northern folk tales but there is nothing particularly improbable in it. Wild boar were still to be found in England at that time. The legend lacks any charms or magic and is really just a straightforward killing of a real animal in an understandable way. There is no absurd elaboration of the ferociousness or size of the boar. Nor, like other dragon killers, does brave Sir Roger gain some fancy reward to end the story in a fairytale way.

There is a general view that 'Brancepeth' is actually derived from 'brawn's path' although there is also a claim that it is named after a Brant family living in that area. The church in Brancepeth is dedicated to the sixth-century Celtic saint St Brandon, and there is another theory that Brancepeth is named after him. There is actually a farm called Brawn's Den just off the Wolsingham Road northwest of Brancepeth.

The story of the Brancepeth Brawn was allegedly authenticated in 1867 when repairs to Cleves Cross Farm revealed the remains of a pit claimed to be that in which the boar had been trapped. Some years earlier on the same farm, a large stone was dug up – said to be all that remained of a cross marking the spot where Sir Roger slew the beast. On the eastern edge of Ferryhill is an area called Cleves Cross, and near a bus stop is the stump of the medieval Cleves Cross. There was a stone plaque there to commemorate this: 'The large stone just above ye part of Cleves Cross marks the site where by tradition the Brawn of BRANCEPETH was killed by ROGER de FERY about the year 1200.'

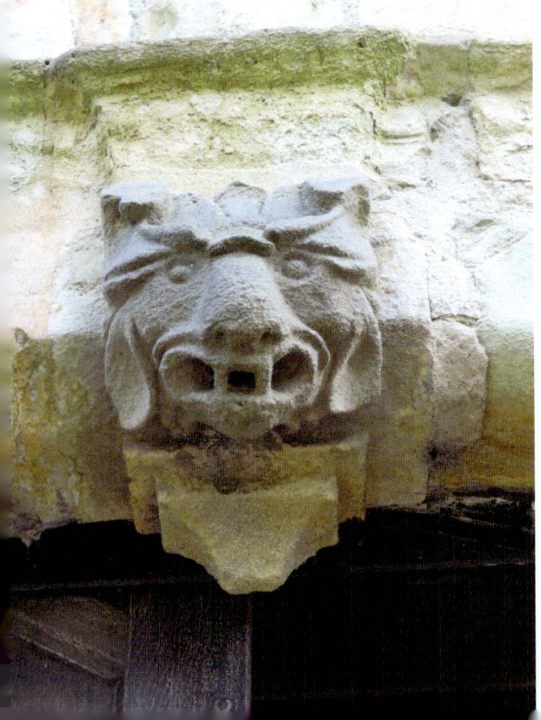

Above the porch of St Brandon's Church in Brancepeth is this not-very-convincing carved boar's head. The splendid woodwork inside the church was, sadly, destroyed by fire. It dated from the reign of John Cosin, Bishop of Durham in the Restoration period. Cosin was very much a ritualist and conservative. He was responsible for a distinctive style of church woodwork and the revival of old traditions.

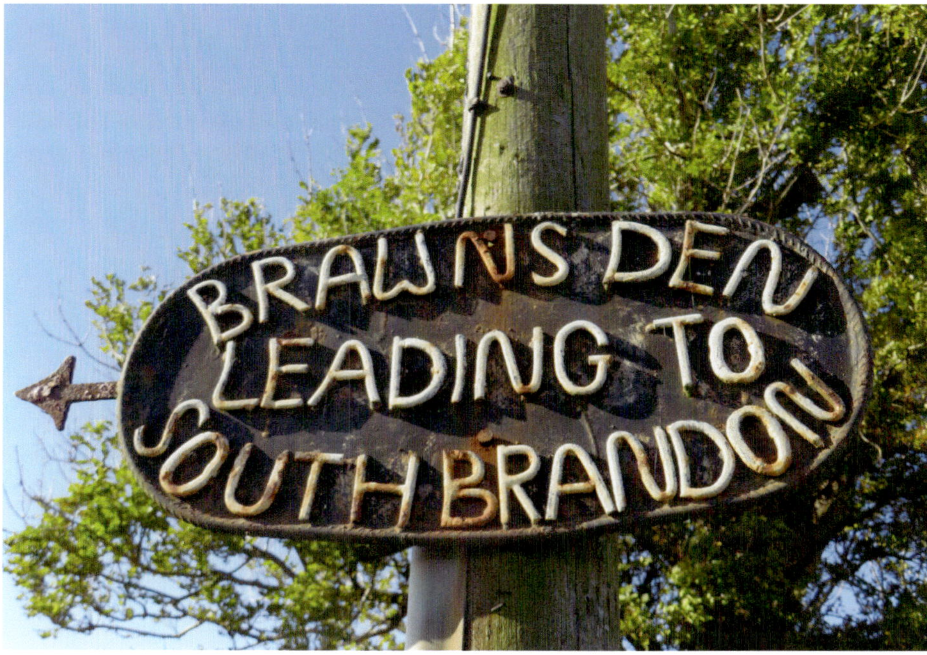

The Brawn's Den Farm sign near Brancepeth and Brandon. These are all names which are claimed to originate from the story of the giant brawn killed by courageous Roger de Ferie, whose name may also be the origin of the name Ferryhill.

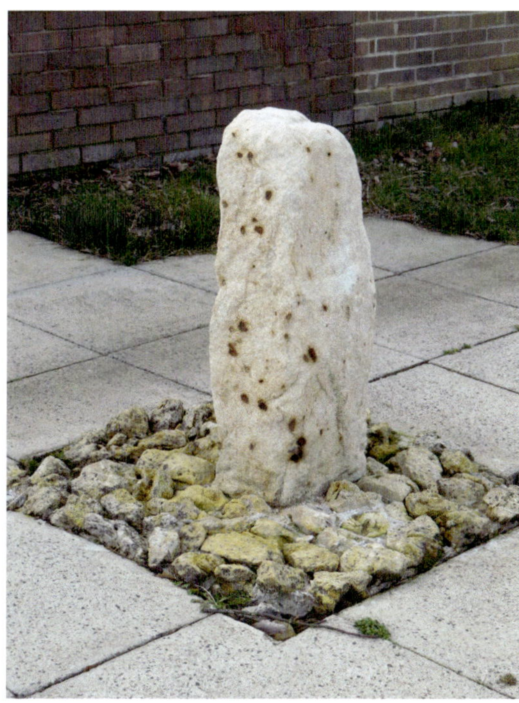

The medieval Cleve's Cross stump still stands in the Cleve's Cross area where many street names commemorate the story as well.

A replica has gone but the original is in the wall of Ferryhill Town Hall. A stained-glass window unveiled before the gaze of Tony Blair, MP for Sedgefield, also commemorates the deed. According to Surtees, the seals of the de Fery family in that era do show a boar. The year 1208 often crops up when there was a knight named Roger de Fery. It is claimed that he is actually buried in Merrington churchyard beneath a coffin shaped gravestone adorned with images of a sword and a spade but the table gravestones are too badly eroded now to identify anything.

There is another wild brawn story associated with an area known as Pollard's Lands on the eastern side of the Gaunless, now part of Bishop Auckland. This boar devastated that part of the bishop's estate around Evenwood and Copley so much that the Bishop of Durham offered a reward for its killing. It was slain by a Richard Pollard who was, apparently, a sharp-witted young man in the service of the Prince Bishop.

Pollard realised the beast was especially fond of roaming in a certain wood, consuming the beech mast which fell from a particular tree. He climbed into the branches and shook down mast onto the ground below. Then he hid in the foliage. Eventually the boar appeared, gorged itself on beech mast then fell

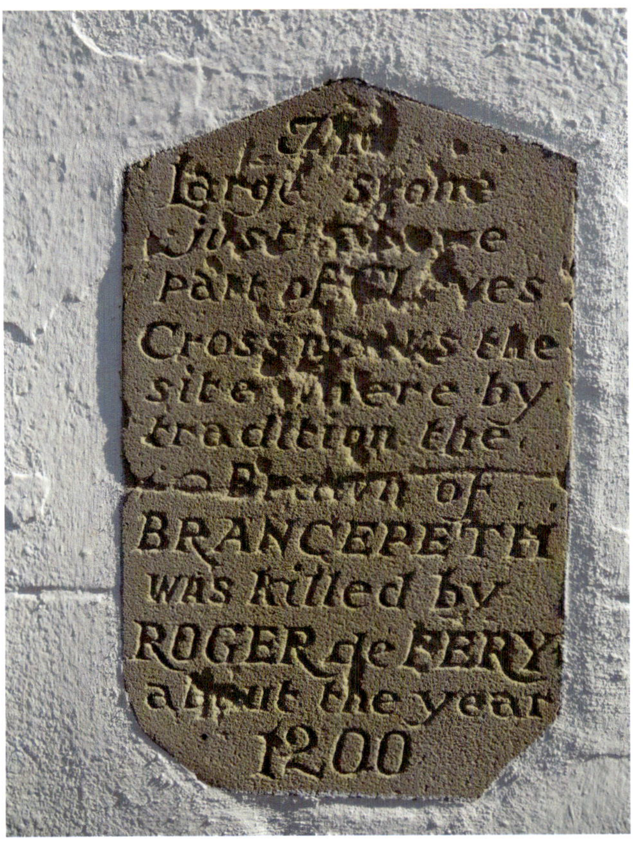

The medieval plaque from Cleve's Cross is now built into the wall of Ferryhill Town Hall.

A detail from the splendid stained-glass window in Ferryhill Town Hall by Tony Steele. The window was unveiled by the Rt Hon. Anthony Blair MP for Sedgefield.

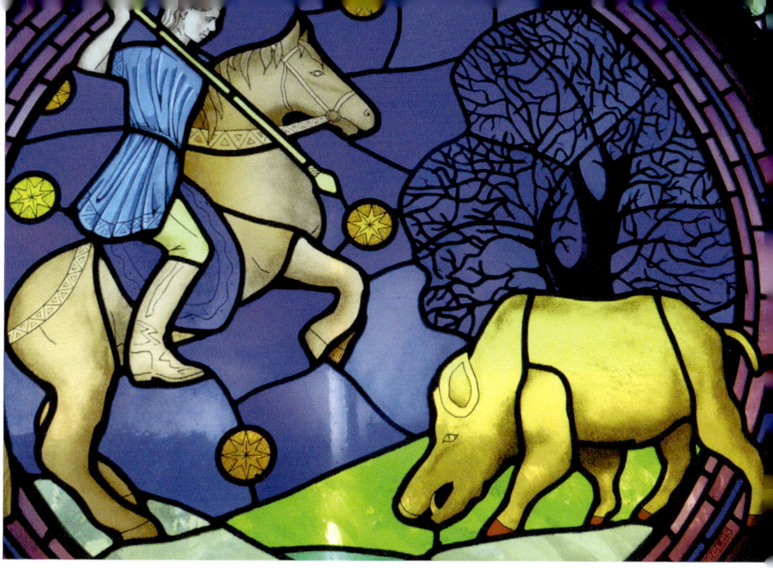

St John's Church at Kirk Merrington is where Roger de Ferie is claimed to be buried beneath a coffin-shaped grave cover.

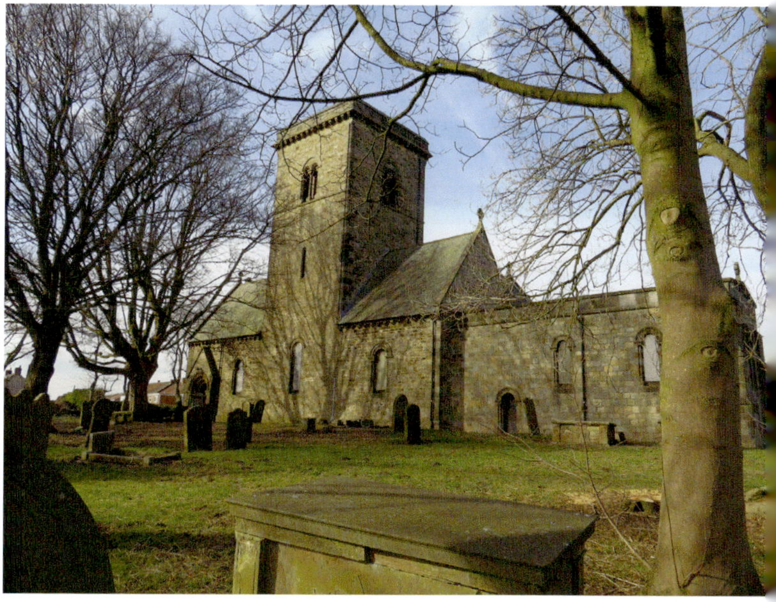

Auckland Palace above the Wear was the seat of power of the prince bishops. Pollard had the brass nerve to claim it all for killing the brawn!

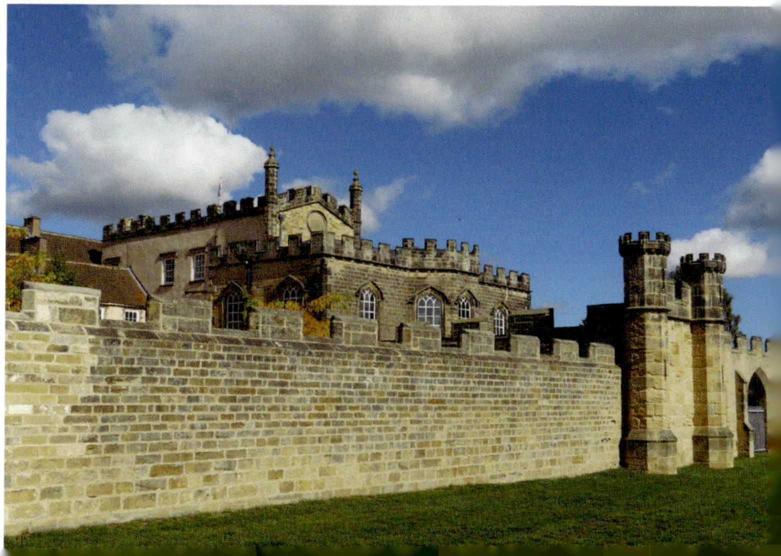

asleep. This was the moment that Pollard had been waiting for. Slipping down, he attacked the monster. For hours the battle raged. Only when dawn came did Pollard deliver the killing blow. According to some versions, he was so exhausted that he fell asleep, and the carcass was stolen by a couple of men passing by. They took it to the bishop and claimed the reward. Fortunately, Pollard had had the wits to cut out the tongue of the boar before he slept so he was able to prove that it was he who should be rewarded.

The delighted bishop offered as a reward as much land Pollard could ride around while the bishop dined. In some accounts the quick-witted young man appeared ten minutes later having ridden around the bishop's estate and claimed his palace and grounds. The amused bishop awarded the young soldier rich land on the north side of Bishop Auckland. This story may be one of those justifying why a local family should enjoy property rights and superiority over their neighbours as with the stories about dragon killers.

The story, though, has an unusual twist. There are also accounts of a wyrm near Bishop Auckland. The fullest account is in *The Works of Sir Walter Scott* Volume III (1806) where Scott talks about a knight slaying a worm at Bishop Auckland. Scott quotes *Fragmenta antiquitatis: or, Ancient tenures of land, and jocular customs of manors* which dates from the early seventeenth century. He attributes the killing to the Pollard family whose lands are held because their

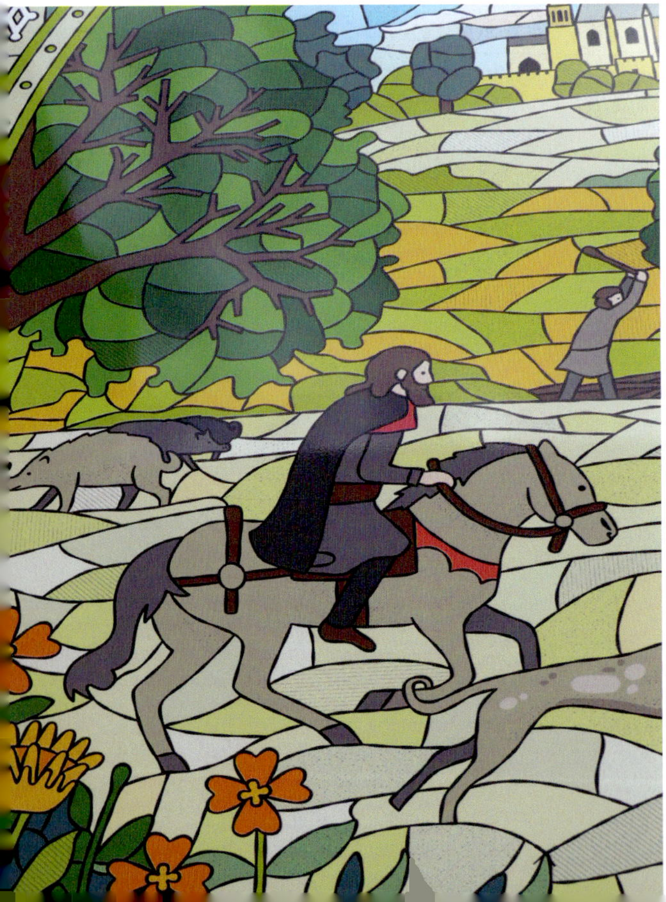

One of a sequence of nine panels outside the Auckland Project Information Centre showing boar hunting. These were designed by James Gibbs and unveiled in 2024.

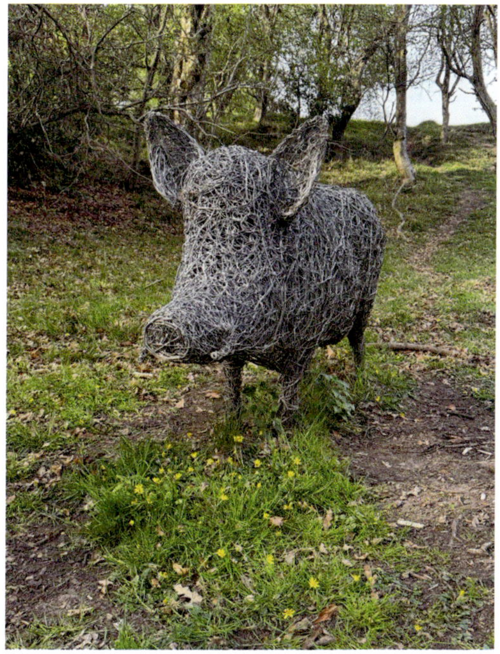

The life-sized wire boar sculpture in Auckland Park by Emma Stothard was installed in 2014. He answers to Bosley Boar if you can find him. (Photograph by William Jones)

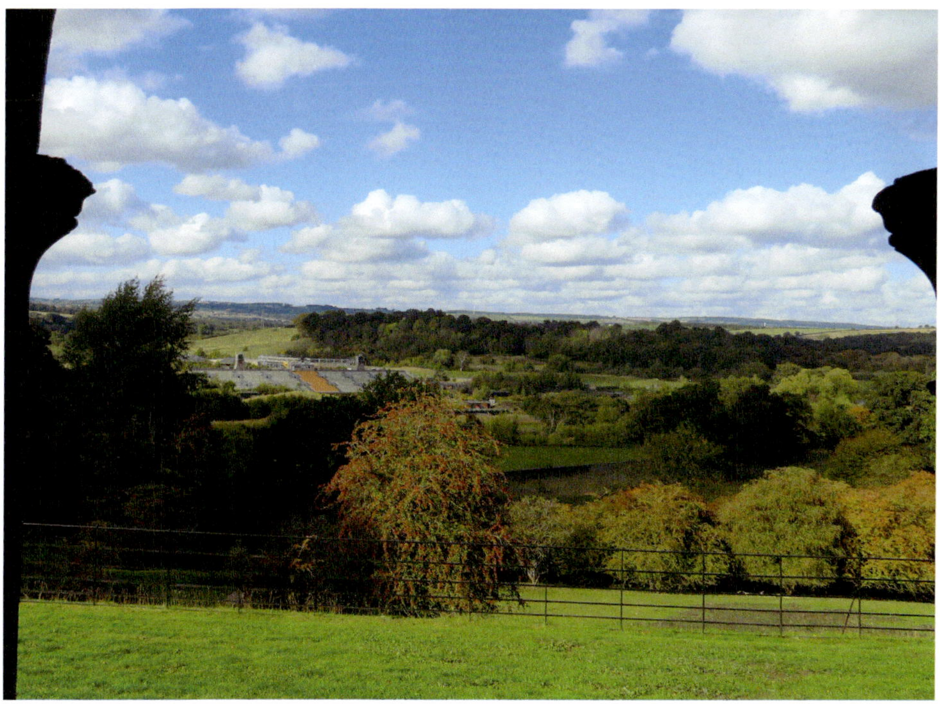

View from Auckland Castle towards the north where the Kynren, a spectacular open-air 'epic tale of England', is held annually. Some of Pollard's lands, including Bishop Auckland Golf Course, are to the right. He wasn't a member of course.

ancestor 'slew of old a great and venomous serpent, which did much harm to man and beast'. That account refers to 1399 as the date when a John Pollard died, when his land was held even then on the basis of Falchion swapping. Yet the *Parliamentary Surveys of the Bishopric of Durham 1649–1650* says: 'The owners of the land are to doe at every Bishop's first coming to be Bishop here to present him with the Falchion with which the Bore was slayne.'

Were two dragons killed in close proximity by different knights, resulting in a near-identical sword-surrendering tradition? Or was one of the beasts killed actually a gigantic boar, but resulting in the same tradition? Of course, the word 'wyrm' merely means vermin, and could be applied to any sort of threatening pest. It may just be a semantic issue which is at the heart of this matter. Anyhow dragons are dragons, and boars are certainly boars, but dragons can be a bigger tourist attraction than boars, you'll agree!

The name Pollard was certainly associated with the Bishop Auckland area at least from the 1240s. In medieval times 'Pollard's Lands' were considered to be a separate manor, and included what is now Bishop Auckland Golf Course, as well as land in the Etherley Moor area. In St Andrew's Church in Bishop Auckland a thirteenth-century wooden effigy is supposedly Sir Richard Pollard, although there is nothing to identify him as such. Admittedly there is what appears to be a boar at his feet, which is unusual, but there are claims that it was originally a lion and was reshaped into a boar.

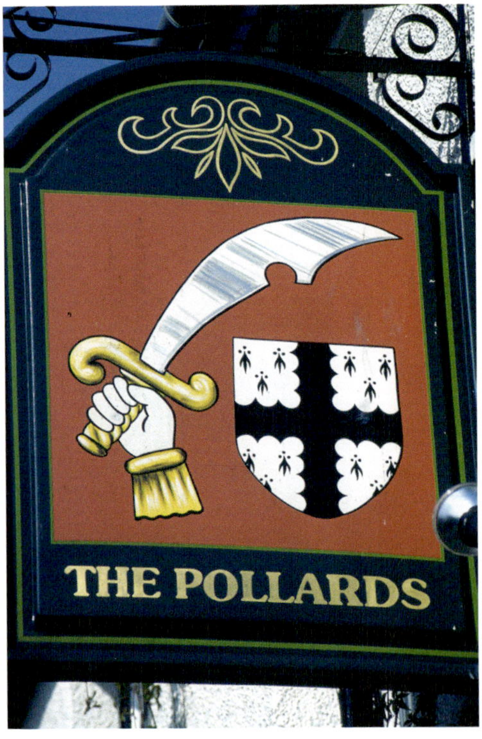

The Pollard's Inn, Etherley Lane, displays a sort of falchion on its sign. You must remember that one version of the story has a wyrm being killed by Pollard and a falchion being exchanged as at Sockburn. I suspect that the artist just picked it out of a catalogue though.

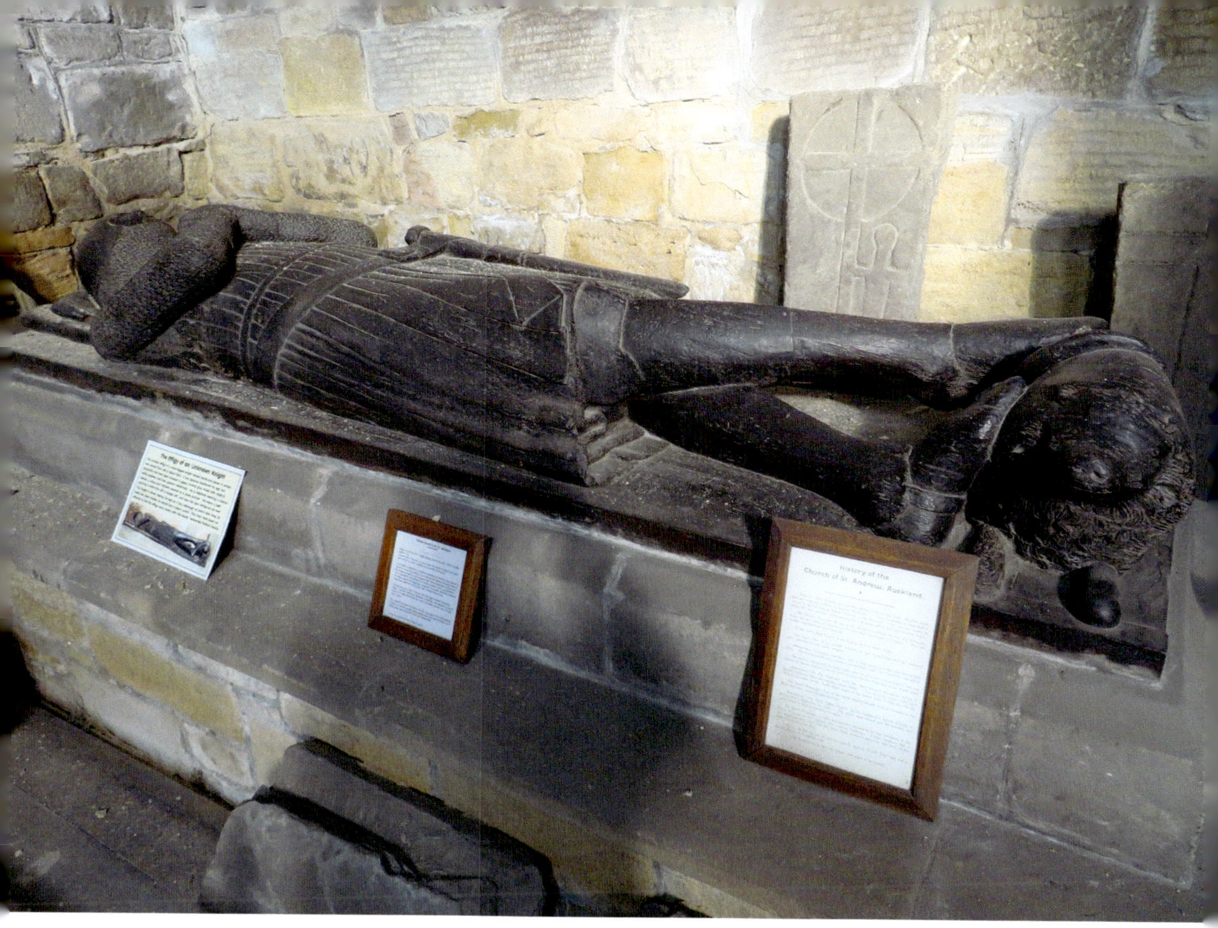

The plaque says 'An Effigy of an Unknown Knight' in St Andrews in South Church, Bishop Auckland. It is said, however, to be Richard Pollard. At his feet is what seems to be a boar. Cynics suggest it was originally a lion but was adapted to resemble a boar. The splendid woodwork in the church, and this unusual wooden effigy, dates from the time of Bishop John Cosin. That man again!

The earliest version of the Pollard story seems to be in the *Parliamentary Surveys*. The use of the Falchion as an emblem in the arms of the family goes back to the fourteenth century. The Pollards died out but in the 1660s the Bishop of Durham, John Cosin, decreed that the freeholders of their former lands were to continue the tradition of presenting the Falchion. This may have been to do with romanticisation of the past or the reclaiming of confiscated land and property rights by linking it to ancient, albeit unprovable, traditions. In both the cases of the Sockburn Wyrm and the Pollard Brawn, the presentation of a sword might be merely a recognition of landholding in the form of a peppercorn rent.

The exploits of Pollard and Ferry are tales of intrepid men who successfully seized an opportunity. Indeed, the world of folk tales is full of men on the make who 'come good' in the end, albeit helped, to some extent, by a stroke of luck.

3
Men on the Make

My first 'man on the make' is a classic example of the genre.

John Duck's birth and parentage are unknown. He arrived in Durham in 1655 and sought apprenticeship as a butcher but the Butcher's Guild warned against taking him on. In one of the old books of the Incorporated Company of Butchers of the City of Durham is the following:

> Md. (Memorandum) that on Tuesday the 12th January, 1656-1657 being one of the quarter meetinge dayes, Robert Blunt and Clement Ladler, wardens of this Company of Butchers, gave John Heslopp warning that from henceforth hee forbear to sett John Ducke on work in the trade of butcher upon payne default 39s,11d.' [*sic*]

No one would employ him because he could not give any details of his place of birth. However, literally from out of the blue, he enjoyed remarkable good fortune. As Duck wandered dejectedly through the streets, a raven dropped a gold Jacobus (a gold coin from the reign of James I) at his feet. On the basis of that he went on to make his fortune. He became one of the wealthiest men in Durham, owning land and collieries in the area.

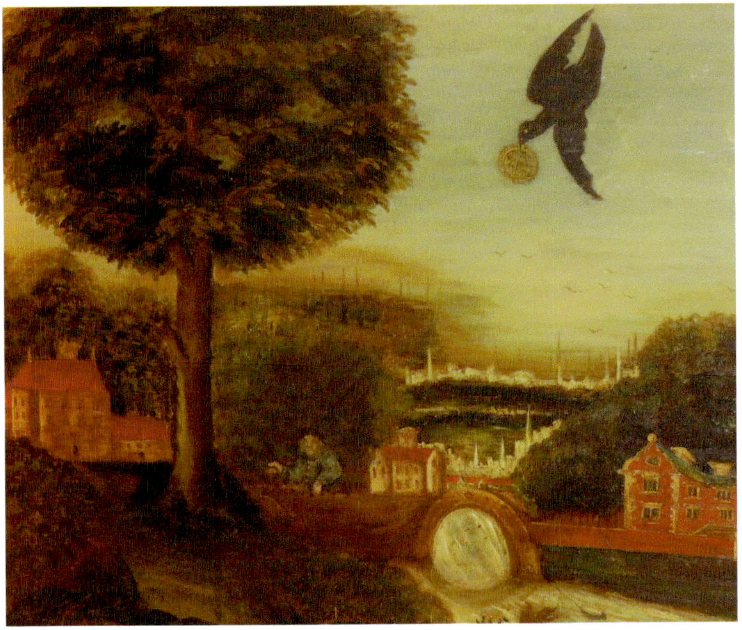

This unusual painting of the Sir John Duck story was discovered in 1963 behind a café's panelling. It is now on a wall in the Drunken Duck in Claypath, formerly the Sir John Duck. Nothing seems to be known about the date or the artist.

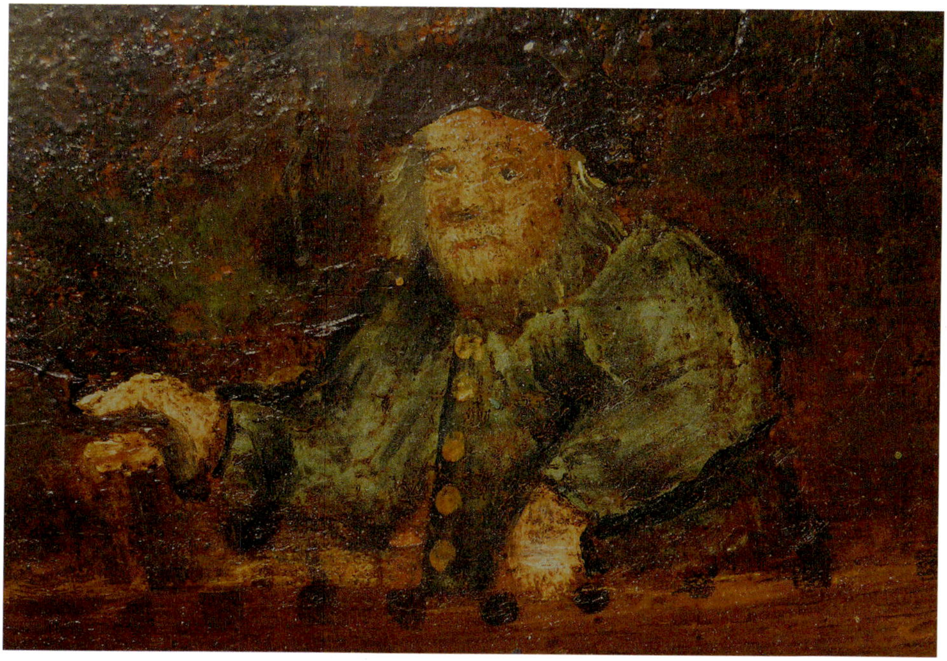

Sir John Duck himself, as shown in this detail from the painting uncovered in 1963 in Luke's Café in Silver Street.

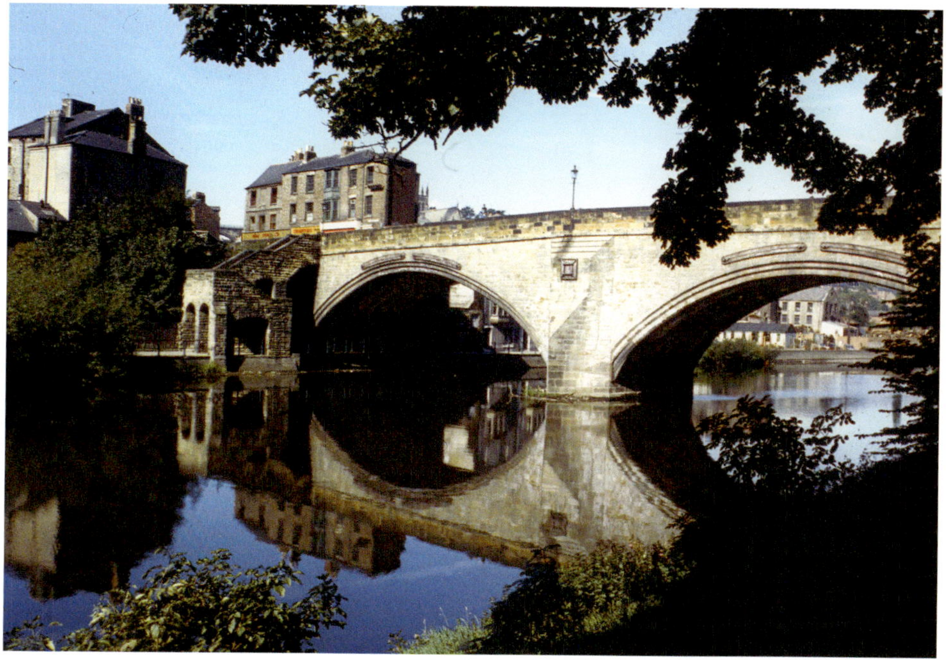

The fifteenth-century Framwellgate Bridge where John Duck received from the heavens the unexpected BACS money transfer which was the basis of his fortune.

He built a great mansion in Silver Street and endowed a hospital for the 'sustenance and relief of 12 poor and impotent widows' at Great Lumley in 1686. In 1665 he married either the sister or daughter of Heslop in St Nicholas in Durham, and the estate of Haswell became his. In 1680 he became Mayor of Durham and progressed to the rank of a baronet becoming Sir John Duck of Haswell on the Hill. At that time, he was also admitted to the Butchers' Company. The record of his admission is as follows: 'John Duck, esq., Mayor of the city of Durham, is admitted with the consent of the Company a freeman of the Fraternity of Butchers, and have paid for such his said admission 13s. 4d.'

Duck died without heirs and was buried in St Margaret of Antioch Church in Durham on 31 August 1691. The Haswell estate was sold by Lady Duck in 1695 and she died on 14 December 1695. The hospital was demolished in 1960, but the site is marked by a very elaborate ornamental wooden bench. The Silver Street house, which was Luke's Café from 1943 to 1963, was demolished in 1963 and a painting was found behind panels over the fireplace which shows the raven with the coin, John Duck by the river and his mansions in the background. It is now in the safe care of the owner of the Drunken Duck (formerly the Sir John Duck) in Durham.

There is a similar story in Newcastle. Roger Thornton, the son of a peasant, became incredibly wealthy from mining, trade and money lending, served three times as Mayor of Newcastle and represented it in Parliament. He was remembered for his liberality and his remarkable Flemish monumental brass is in Newcastle Cathedral. Of course, Duck and Thornton will remind you of Dick Whittington and his remorseless rise to become Lord Mayor of London four times. The reason for the plethora of stories of likely lads doing well against adversity was the opportunities opened by the Black Death and subsequent waves of plague for ambitious men of lowly backgrounds, and the growing admiration for these Gordon Geckos of the Middle Ages.

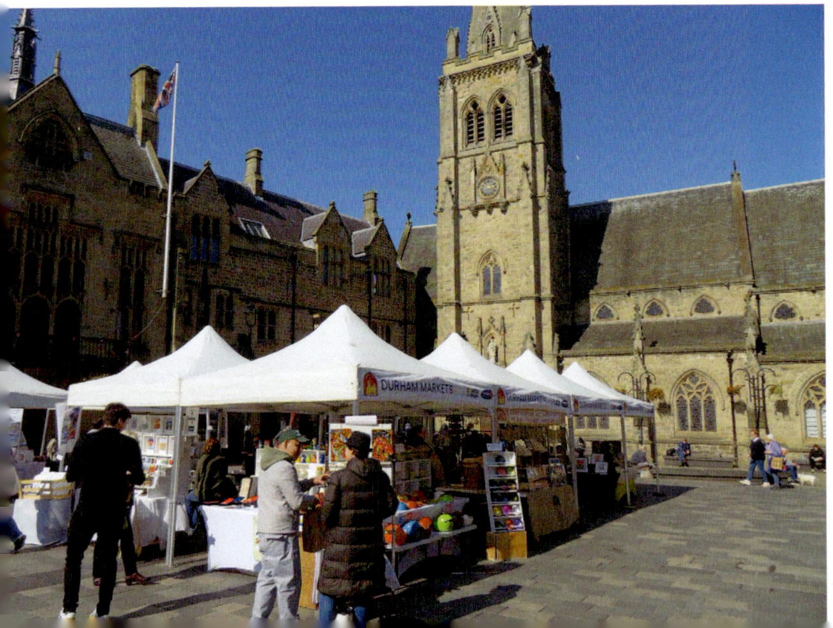

Durham Town Hall and the Guild Hall, with St Nicholas' Church seen across Durham marketplace. Duck was married in the church and became a prominent civic dignitary and butcher.

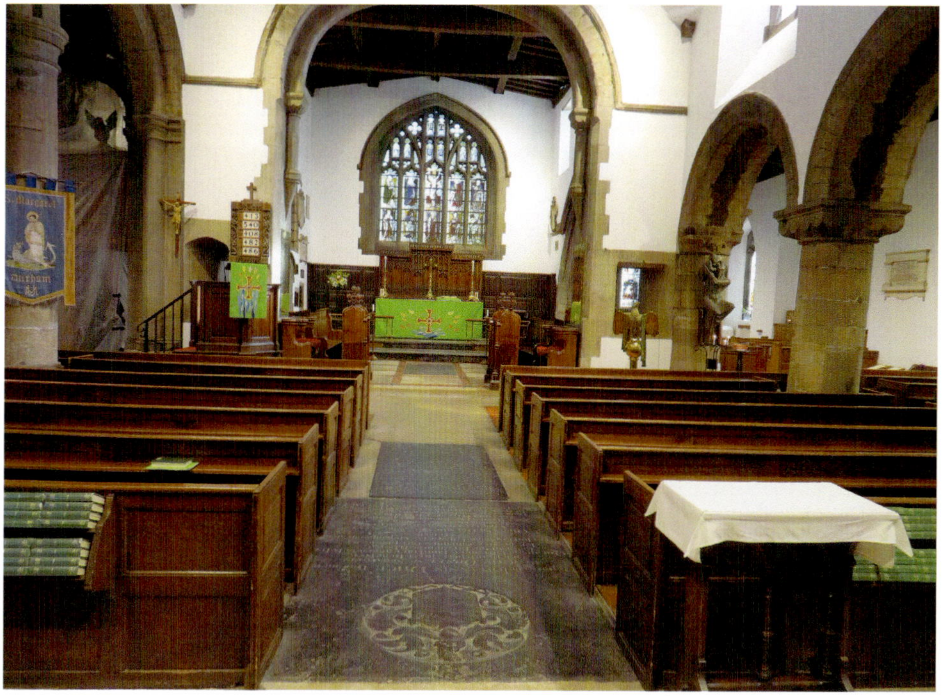

St Margaret's of Antioch in Crossgate. The burial place of Sir John Duck is marked by a large ledger slab in the nave. St Margaret was famously once swallowed by a dragon but escaped because her cross triggered an explosive intestinal reaction. She would have felt at home in dragon-infested County Durham then.

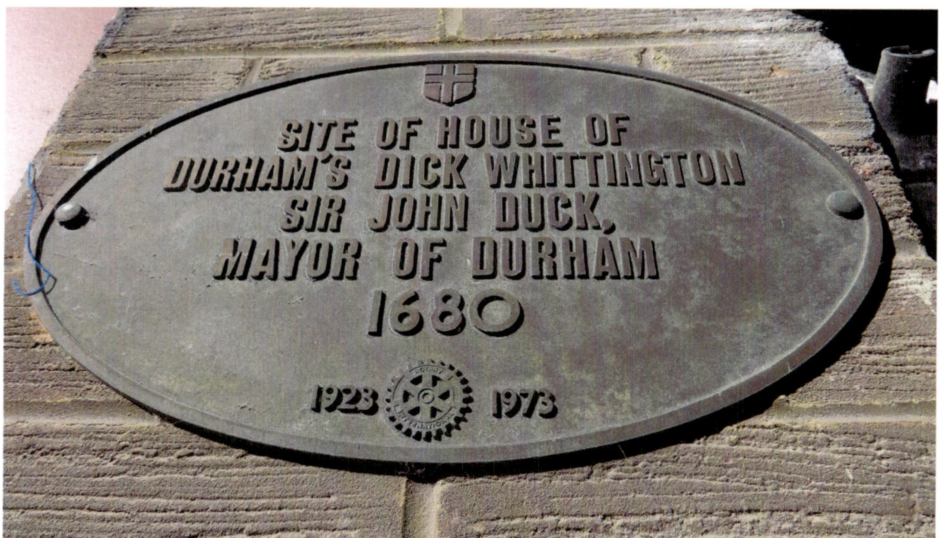

The Sir John Duck plaque on the wall of No. 39 Silver Street, where his mansion was until 1963 and where the painting was uncovered when Luke's Café closed.

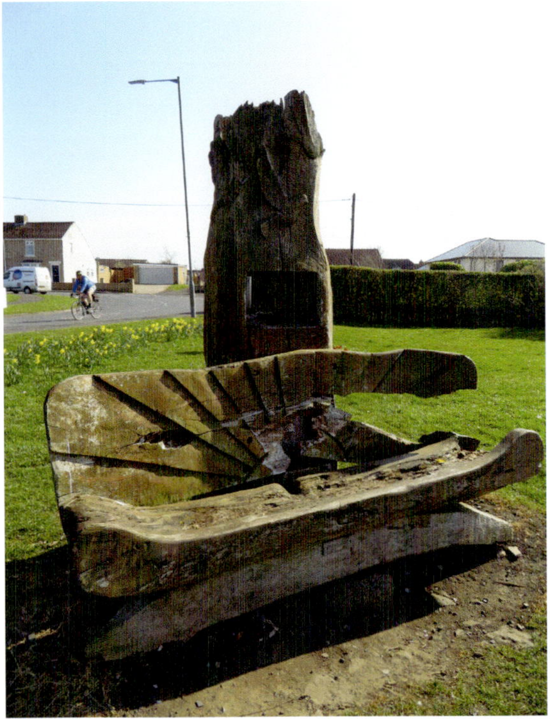

The uncomfortable wooden bench which is the memorial to the hospital almshouses of Sir John Duck and wife. They have been demolished but stood in the Back Lane at Great Lumley overlooking Chester-le-Street.

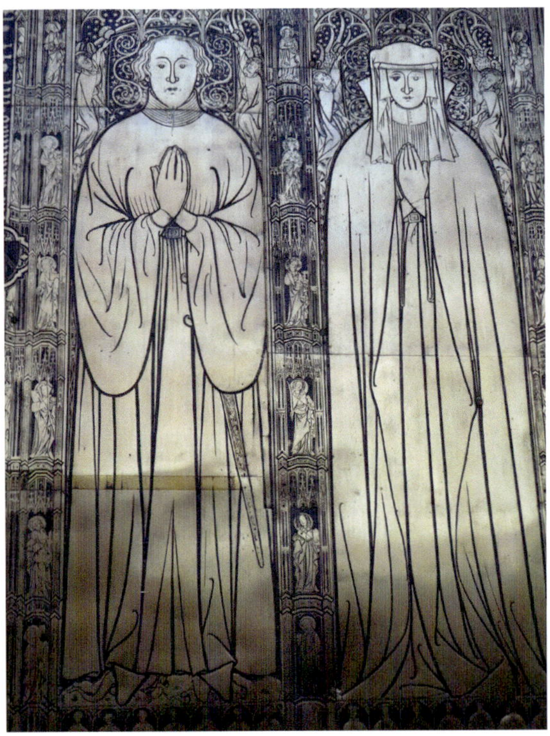

The monumental brass of Roger and Agnes Thornton in St Nicholas' Cathedral in Newcastle. Thornton was another of those Dick Whittington types, although, like Whittington, he didn't actually make his way up from poverty as Duck seems to have done.

Then there are those ambitious men who pursue dangerous careers as highwaymen. In Ryhope there is a persistent tale that Dick Turpin was active in the area and haunted Ryhope Hall whose lady was his lover and protectress. According to a *Sunderland Echo* article dated 31 March 1932, Turpin 'occasionally visits in spirit what was a favourite halting place in his northern journeys'. In fact, Ryhope Hall was another name for a now-demolished inn called the Three Boars Head and 'Lady Lowther' was no 'Lady' but a long-time brassy publican. There is no evidence at all that Turpin made his way to Ryhope, or beyond Beverley where he was eventually arrested for horse stealing. The story probably arises from confusion with a real highwayman.

Robert Drummond was born in 1680, or thereabouts. He claimed that he was descended from a titled Scottish family although it was almost obligatory for highwaymen to claim gentry backgrounds. He went into the hardware line, dealing in razors, knives, thimbles and such-like, and eventually settled in Sunderland. According to Hayward in his *Lives of the Most Remarkable Criminals* his daily trade masked a violent night-time reality leading to transportation after a failed housebreaking venture. However, he returned to England and embarked on a crime spree. In reality, Drummond, like Turpin, appears to have been a violent thug. He fell in with the cousins Ferdinando and William Shrimpton and they were captured after a series of nasty incidents on Hounslow Heath.

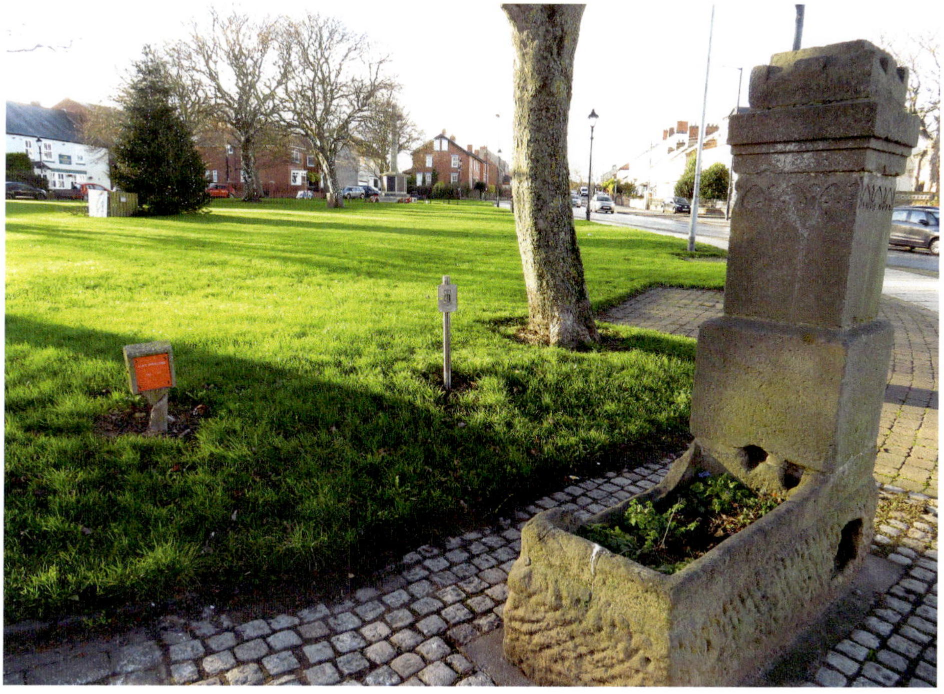

Ryhope village green may once have encountered the clattering hooves of Dick Turpin's steed as he sought to visit his noble ladylove. Or then again, perhaps not.

William turned king's evidence, and Drummond and Ferdinando were sentenced to death. According to Hayward, the pair died with a display of bravado as they embarked upon the Tyburn jig:

> They valued blood no more than they did water, but were ready to shed the first with as little concern as they spilt the latter. Inured in wickedness and rapine, old in years and covered in offences, they yielded their last breaths at Tyburn, with very little sign of contrition or repentance, on the 17th of February, 1730, Drummond being about fifty, and Shrimpton about thirty years of age.

Elsewhere, in Washington, it is believed that a curse hangs over a former smithy, which is now a popular restaurant. A highwayman called Robert Hazlett, it is said, placed a curse on all its owners. Thus, there have been frequent power cuts for no apparent reason. A ghost who can find the trip switch seems a rather unlikely type but it takes all sorts. Hazlett was real enough though. Robert Hazlett (or Hazlitt) alias William Hudson of Washington was the first person gibbeted in the North East following the 1752 Murder Act.

His date of birth is unrecorded. He seems to have once been a clerk of a wealthy merchant in London then became a highwayman in the south of England. In the North East he operated on Gateshead Fell, open marshland south of Gateshead, crossed by the main road from Durham to Newcastle. On this desolate moorland, Hazlett struck twice one evening. His first victim was wealthy spinster Miss Margaret Benson of Newcastle. Hazlett was said to have put a pistol to her head and demanded her purse and her watch. Far from being Claude Duval, our hero was 'trembling from head to foot'. Cursing him she gave him half a guinea. The other victim was postman William Roper carrying two sacks of cheques and other valuables. Hazlett demanded them and flourished a pistol.

Unfortunately, a small boy was out walking. He recognised the horse, a grey mare, which he had seen the week before at the blacksmiths in Washington village. The precocious child hastened to the constables of Gateshead. The Washington blacksmith confirmed that he had a customer every Friday with a grey mare. The next Friday the constables waited in the shed. Hazlett sought to escape but the constables seized him, searched his saddle bags, and found his pistol and black mask. Tried, found guilty and hanged, his body was then taken to a gibbet erected near the place where the robberies were committed. By unfortunate coincidence, he had once robbed the judge who tried him!

Sunderland therefore does have a claim to having two actual highwaymen. Both of them are ghosts and neither lived up to Turpin's glamorised version – nor did Turpin for that matter. Both are examples of the way in which reality can be embroidered to enhance the appeal.

An even more striking example are Burke and Hare, the Irish 'resurrectionists' who hold such a grip on the Sunderland imagination. According to the popular website *Sunderland Online*, Burke and Hare began their partnership by selling hot

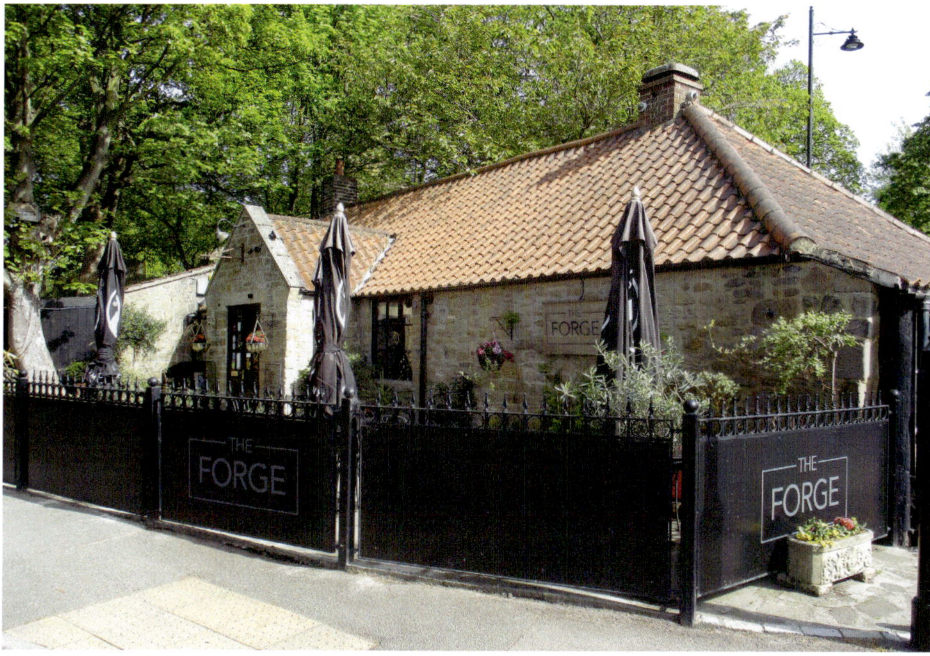

The Forge restaurant in Washington is a former blacksmith's. The building is 400 years old and witnessed the capturing of the highwayman (and amateur electrician) Robert Hazlett, following information from a roaming eagle-eyed child.

pies to the navvies of Sunderland: 'In the cold white winter of 1824, Sunderland heard the shouts of two men selling their hot food. One short and stocky called William Burke, the other tall and slim named William Hare. These two men, originally from Ireland, soon became famous body snatchers.'

According to this, and other popular sources, Burke and Hare were labouring on the construction of a new pier. The *Newcastle Weekly Chronicle* (Vol. 2, No. 13, March 1888) remarks about this: 'Burke, it was said, worked some time at Sunderland as a labourer while the piers were building. Hare, it was understood, made his way to Newcastle, where his identity was lost through his changing his name.'

Sadly, there is no evidence that Burke and Hare even visited Sunderland. Sunderland certainly had a growing Irish community but it is clear that the deadly duo did not actually meet until they were both living in Edinburgh. Oddly enough, Great Yarmouth also has a similar Burke and Hare story which would make them very busy Irishmen.

Sunderland did have resurrectionists, but not Burke and Hare. One oft-described case in 1823 made a great sensation. Two Scottish strangers, Thomas Thompson of Dundee and John Weatherley of Renfrew, aroused suspicion because of frequent visits to the churchyard. In the corner of their lodgings they were surprised by a child's corpse, carefully packed up, and addressed to Mr James Jamieson, Leith Street, Edinburgh. Various other items included a record of expenses. They were tried at Durham Sessions and sentenced to three months' imprisonment, with a fine of sixpence each. It's difficult to say which aspect is the most interesting: that the penalty was so modest or that the postal system seemed to be used like Amazon Prime as a carrier of packaged corpses! Thompson and Weatherley are not as eye-catching as Burke and Hare but it is possible that the duos have been switched in popular imagination.

My next story stars another Drummond and a complex and intriguing claim for a lost title. As with the other stories told here, there may well be truth in it.

It all begins at Culloden on Wednesday 16 April 1746. As the Jacobite army lined up, Lord George Murray commanded the right, Lord John Drummond the centre, and his elder brother, the Duke of Perth, the left. At the end of the day, the Jacobite army was routed and Hawley's dragoons began massacring survivors. In fear of their lives, many rebels, including James and John Drummond, sought to flee the country. The brothers boarded a ship for France. James may have been badly injured. The 'official version' is that he died on board ship. The disputed version of events is that the ship docked at South Shields. James went ashore and made his way to South Biddick to 'lie low' because he was attainted under penalty of treason which carried the death sentence. This was not lifted until 1784, two years after he died. James was given refuge by a coal miner called John Armstrong, married Armstrong's daughter Elizabeth in November 1749 and began a career as a ferryman.

Upon the death of James, his son William decided to try and reclaim title and estates. Unfortunately, vital papers had been lost during the wreck of a ship, and others were lost from the boat house in a great flood in 1771. Thomas, a grandson of James, embarked upon legal proceedings in 1826. Finally, the claim was found proven in Scotland, with Thomas proved to be nearest and lawful heir. The restoration of the titles and estates was ordered but this was overturned

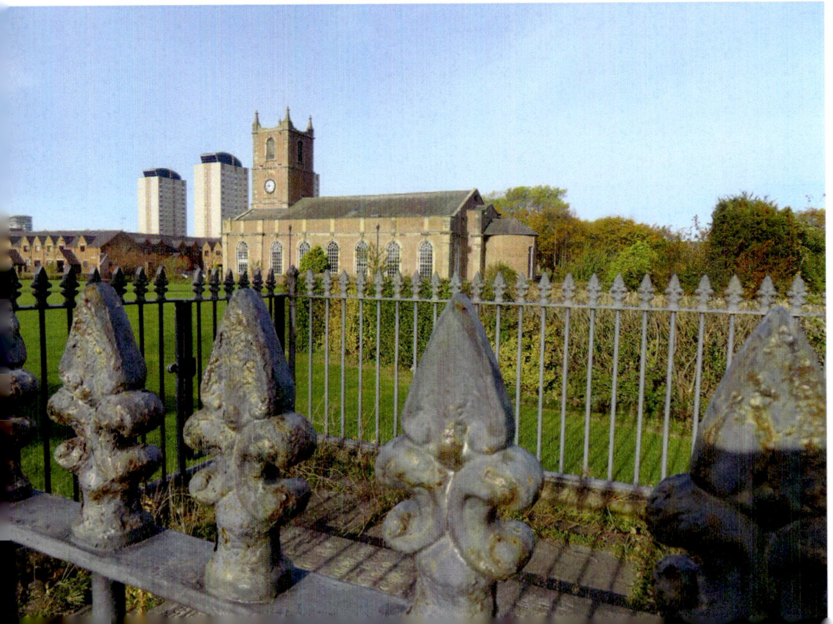

Sunderland graveyard had 100,000 burials between 1719 and 1854. The parish church of Holy Trinity is in the background. If Burke and Hare were active in Sunderland, which they weren't, this would have been a popular place of resort for them.

in January 1835 because of the lapse of time. To this very day, there are still descendants of the Drummonds of Biddick who claim the title of the Duke of Perth. Thomas is buried in the graveyard of Penshaw Church very near the home of the Lambton Worm, which is one of the two songs especially linked to the county. The other is 'Bobby Shafto'.

Near Belsay in Northumberland, there is a famous rock formation known as Shafto Crags. Bobby is said to have sprung from the Ffolliots family, who lived nearby in the fourteenth century and unsurprisingly adopted a name which

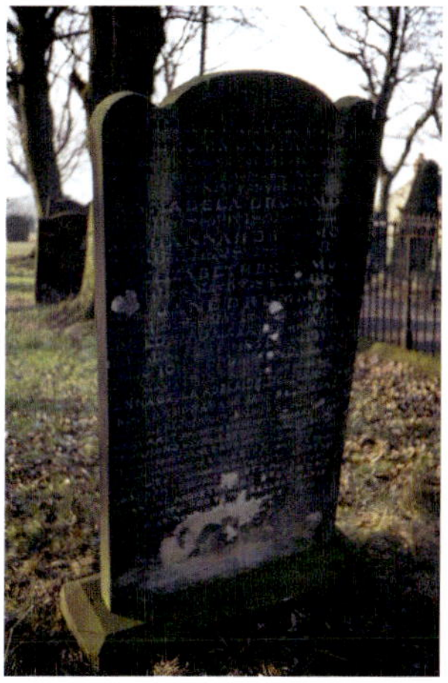

The gravestone of some of the Drummonds of Penshaw at All Saints' Church refers to the 3rd Earl of Perth. It is now broken and faces downward. There are still Drummond descendants to this day who claim the title.

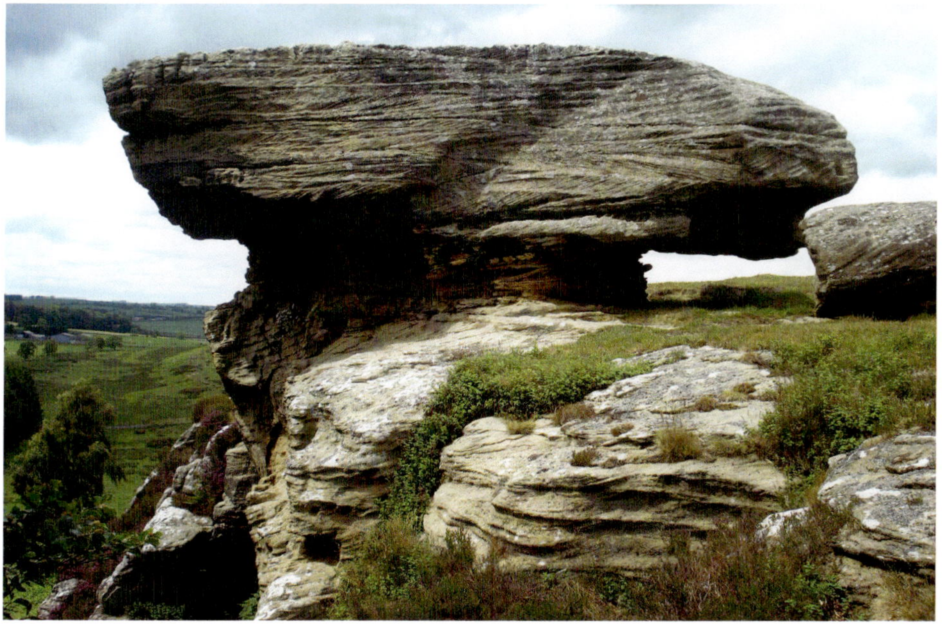

The oddly named Piper's Chair on Shaftoe Crags in Northumberland is in the area where the Shaftos (there are two different spellings used) derived, formerly the Ffolliots.

involved less stuttering. Robert Shafto was born around 1732 at the family seat of Whitworth near Spennymoor, and succeeded to the family estates in 1742. He became one of the two Members of Parliament for County Durham in 1760, using his nickname 'Bonny Bobby Shafto' and the now famous song for electioneering purposes. His undistinguished Parliamentary career ended in 1790. He died in 1797 and is buried in the Shafto family crypt beneath the floor of Whitworth Church.

In 1774, Shafto married Anne Duncombe, daughter and heir of Thomas Duncombe of Duncombe Park, Yorkshire. It is claimed that the news of this marriage (and rapidly 'getten a bairn, For to dandle on his airm') broke the heart of another woman, Bridget Belasyse of Brancepeth Castle, and that she died two weeks later as a result. Thus, the song 'Bobby Shafto' reminds its listeners of the love this woman felt for her silver-buckled, fair-haired gallant.

This can't be true. Bridget died of tuberculosis a fortnight before the wedding. Bobby Shafto never went to sea. The song itself already existed by 1760. The catchy music predates the song so all of the lyrics were later additions. The oldest known version of the tune is dated 1694/95, under the title 'Brave Willie Forster'. Thomas and George Allan, in their *Tyneside Songs and Readings* (1891), argued that the 'Bobby Shafto' of the song was in fact a relative, Robert Shafto of Benwell. None of the likely suspects ever seem to have gone to sea at all. So, despite being the wrong man, the wrong trade, a pirated song and celebrating the jilting of an unhappy young woman, Bobby Shafto continues to be a great north-eastern icon. Even the present-day Whitworth Hall is modern, having been rebuilt in 1900 after a fire. Sometimes it is difficult being a historian!

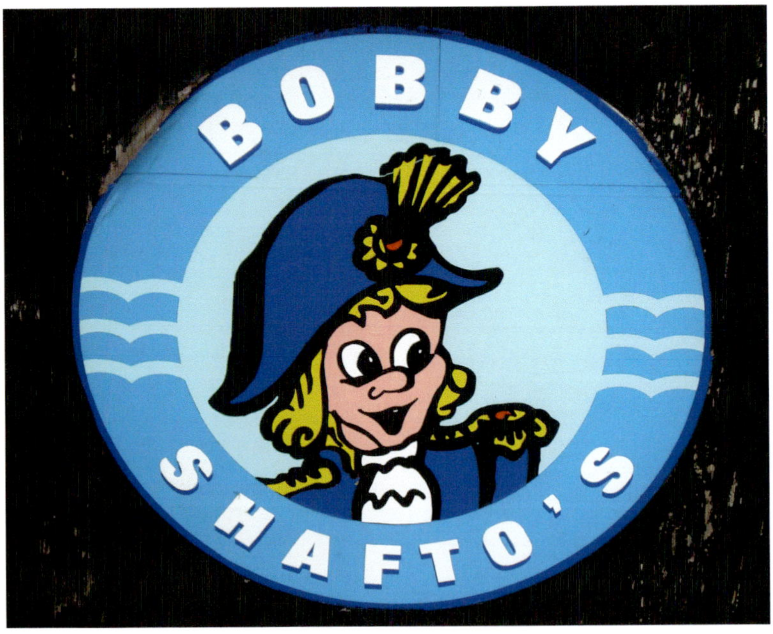

Bobby Shafto would turn over in his grave if he saw this! Although since everything else about him appears to be untrue or imagined, perhaps he is better off as a logo!

4
Ghosties and Ghoulies

Of all the ghost stories of County Durham perhaps the most famous is that of the Cauld Lad of Hylton Castle. The usual version is as follows.

At the beginning of the seventeenth century Sir Robert Hylton employed a stable boy called Roger Skelton. Roger complained of it being cold in the servants' quarters and started to sleep in the warmer stables. One day he overslept and didn't get his master's horse ready on time. The baron flew into a rage and struck the boy with a riding crop or hurled a pitchfork at him. Whichever it was – let's go for both – the poor lad died. Some claim that the baron was so demented that he cut off Roger's head.

This sounds a little extreme and it has been claimed by some that the real crime of the stable boy was that he was embroiled in an affair with the daughter of the baron. Anyhow the baron sought to hide his deed by concealing the body in a well or pond. The body was discovered. Sir Robert was put on trial but got off

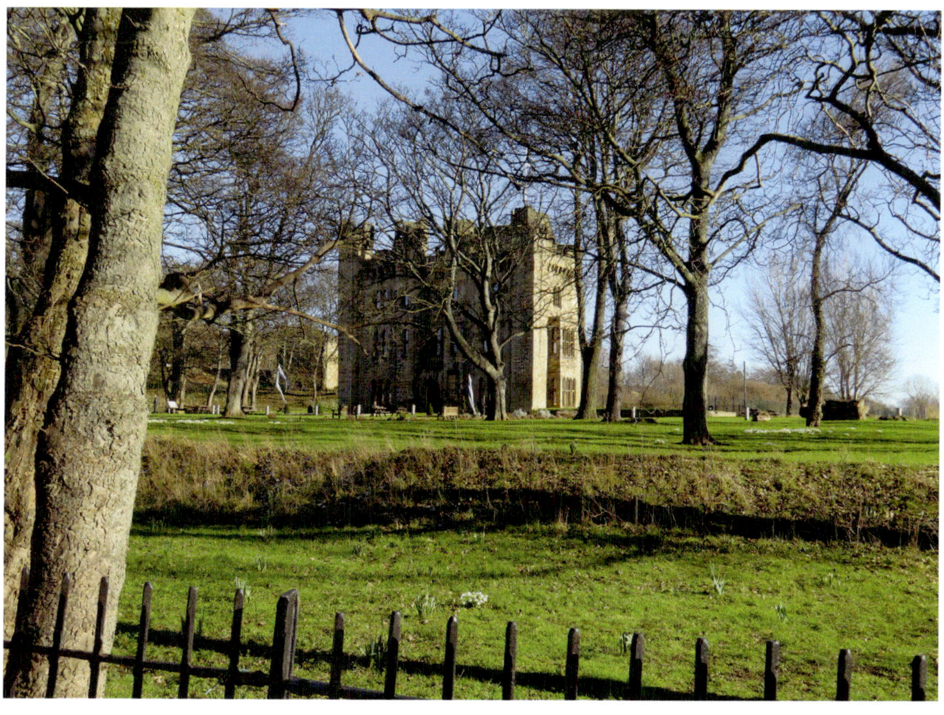

Hylton Castle is a four-storey gatehouse tower. Originally wooden, it was rebuilt in stone in the fourteenth century. It has been restored and is in the care of English Heritage. It is seen here from the south-west from the roadside.

because an old farm worker stated that the baron had ordered the boy to remove a tool from the top shelf in the barn, and the boy had fallen, seriously wounding himself in the process. The baron had actually tended to the wounds, but the boy had died.

Then strange things began to happen. Pots and pans were hurled about and broken. Chamber pots were emptied on the floor. The kitchen was turned upside down. Strange noises were heard and, intriguingly, the shape of a body, made from ashes, would be found on the floor. Sometimes there were more positive occurrences such as the laying out of clothes neatly or tidying up in the kitchen. The servants would often leave out bread or cream as a reward to encourage this rather than all the chamber pot emptying. Life became so uncertain that the cook held a vigil one night to see who was causing the trouble, and saw the spectre of a shivering, naked boy, crying 'I'm cauld! I'm cauld!' So the cook and his wife got a cloak and left it out for the ghost. The next night the ghostbusters saw the spectre happily take up the clothes, proclaiming: 'Here's a cloak and here's a hood, the Cauld Lad of Hylton will do no more good.' And with that he vanished, never to be seen again.

Other versions claim though that the Cauld Lad was never laid to rest and still roams the castle (which is better for the tourist trade). M. A. Richardson wrote in 1843 that the Cauld Lad was still being seen, and singing the following song:

Wae's me, wae's me,*
The acorn's not yet fallen from the tree,
That's to grow the wood,
That's to make the cradle,
That's to rock the bairn
That's to grow to the man
That's to lay me!

* 'Woe is me, woe is me'

Allegedly there have been sightings, and hearings, into the twentieth century.

It may be that the story of the Cauld Lad has become confused with a much older form of folk legend. The spirit may, in fact, have been a fairy or some such sprite, and thus in the wrong chapter! Traditionally a gift of clothes can rid a house of such undesirables. However much you may regard fairy folk as endearingly Enid Blyton-ish they are, in fact, historically less attractive and do little to help property values. You would be well advised to inform your insurer!

Joseph Jacobs in 1890 in his *English Fairy Tales* says the Lad was a brownie 'a funny little thing, half man, half goblin, with pointed ears and hairy hide'. There is a view however that the Cauld Lad was a shape-shifting Barghest. There are lots of them in the north of England. In Yorkshire, one notable case is said to frequent a remote gorge named Troller's Gill. During the 1870s, a Barghest was said to live near Darlington taking the form, variously, of a headless man, a headless lady, a white cat, a rabbit, or a black dog. Barghests can allegedly serve as an omen of death, often by lying across the threshold of the doomed person. If you ever encounter one remember that they cannot cross rivers, if that's any help.

Robert Surtees, in *The Histories and Antiquities of the County Palatinate of Durham,* Volume III says:

> Every castle, tower, or manor-house, has its visionary inhabitants. 'The cauld lad of Hilton' belongs to a very common and numerous class, the Brownie, or domestic spirit; and seems to have possessed no very distinctive attributes. He was seldom seen, but was heard nightly by the servants who slept in the great hall. If the kitchen had been left in perfect order, they heard him amusing himself by breaking plates and dishes, hurling the pewter in all directions, and throwing every thing into confusion. If, on the contrary, the apartment had been left in disarray (a practice which the servants found it most prudent to adopt), the indefatigable goblin arranged every thing with the greatest precision.

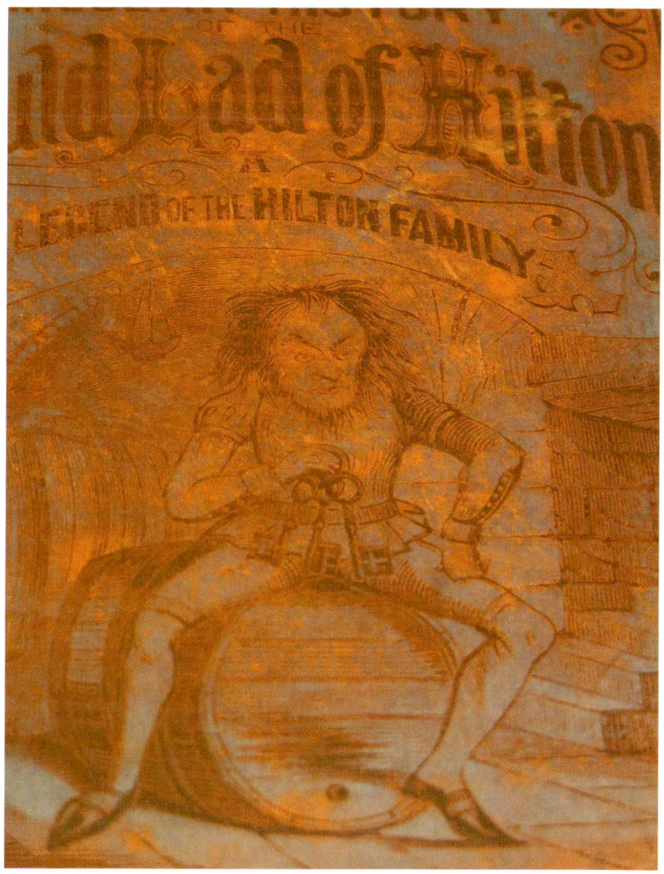

The 'Cauld Lad' as shown on the front cover of a popular cheap booklet.

In fact, Surtees does suggest that there is a sort of collision of two separate folklore traditions, where fairy meets ghost and the two become one. Then the latter format takes over and becomes dominant from the later eighteenth century and throughout the nineteenth century when ghost stories were becoming more popular in romantic Gothic literature.

There is actually evidence that on 3 July 1609 a servant boy was found dead and Sir Robert Hylton, the 13th Baron, was charged with manslaughter using a scythe. A verdict of accidental death was returned since the Baron had been mowing the grass and accidentally cut the leg of the boy. Sir Robert was granted a free pardon by Bishop James on 6 September 1609.

The Hylton title dated back to 1295 but the first creation fell into abeyance in 1746. A first castle, built in about 1072, was subsequently rebuilt in stone by Sir William Hylton (1376–1435) as a four-storey, gatehouse-style, fortified manor house. The building underwent major changes in the eighteenth century. Today the castle is owned by English Heritage. Since 2016, with the benefit of £2.9 million Heritage Lottery funding, it has been superbly restored and turned into a community facility and visitor attraction.

One of the other great visitor attractions in the area is Marsden Bay in South Tyneside. It was long renowned for smugglers as the caves there could be used for storing contraband. From the late eighteenth century a veritable honeycomb

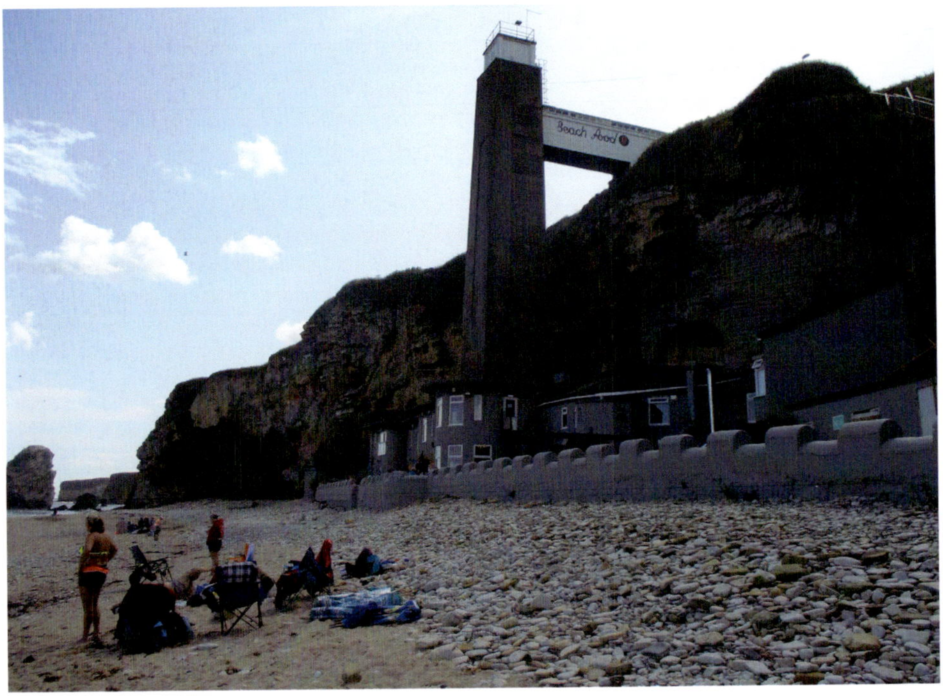

The lift to Marsden Grotto was installed in 1938 by Vaux Brewery. The hotel is within the cave complex, which was created in the eighteenth and nineteenth centuries.

of caves was deliberately excavated by former Allenhead miner Jack Bates, the so-called 'Jack the Blaster', and his successor Peter Allan from East Lothian. Originally for residential purposes, the grotto became a tourist attraction. It is now a hotel and restaurant. It also has two ghosts.

To the south of the Grotto, Peter drove a shaft to help bring goods down. It became known as the Smugglers' Hole because it was believed to be haunted by a smuggler, Jack the Jibber, who had 'jibbed' (betrayed) his companions. Suspended in a tub, he was let down only once every day to receive food scraps and jeers from his fellows. Even worse was that he was able to witness his comrades feasting and he would then be pelted with the bones. It is said that his moans and sighs can still be heard. It's the wind actually! Apart from the moaning of the snitch, the grotto has the ghost of a smuggler who walked in for a drink after a hard day's work. A soldier entered and the smuggler struck him believing he was about to arrest him. The soldier pursued him and shot him in the back. The landlord took the man's tankard and nailed it onto the rock around the bar pronouncing that it was cursed and that anyone who drank from it would be the victim of evil. It is claimed that the ghost has been seen frequently, and that drink left in the tankard overnight is gone by the next morning. Well, it would, wouldn't it!

Not far from Marsden is Cleadon Mill perched on its splendid vantage point with a panoramic view of the region. This was once the home of Elizabeth Gibbon, daughter of Thomas, the owner of the mill. She fell deeply in love with a smuggler, named by some as Peter the Pirate. Thomas was horrified and forbade

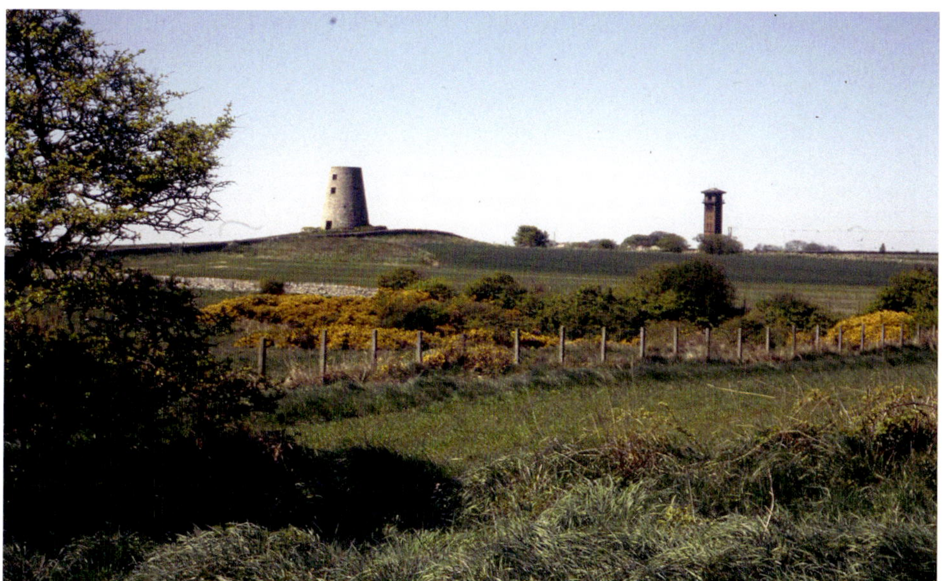

Cleadon Mill in South Shields, where the broken-hearted Elizabeth Gibbon died by suicide. You can understand why her father didn't want her to marry a man called Peter the Pirate though!

her to see him again. As time passed by, her broken heart caused her great depression. One day, when she could take no more, she climbed to the top of the mill in her red dress and threw herself off. The ghost of the so-called Red Lady is said to haunt the mill until this very day, seen by many dog walkers and hikers.

Now head along the very busy A1231 to bustling Chester-le-Street on our ghost hunt. Another tormented soul haunts the Lumley Castle Hotel, which is renowned for Medieval Feast entertainments. It is also the home of an apparition called Lily. She was secretly married to Ralph Lumley, the builder of the castle, who served under the tyrannical King Richard II. Legend has it that two murderous priests threw poor Lily down the well to save her soul for having converted to Protestantism. Some versions say this happened in 1390 but that is long before Protestantism made an appearance. Of course, when Ralph returned, the fact that his wife had disappeared would be a problem, so the priests said she had gone into a convent! You can still see the well in the castle grounds and the ghost is said to float up from the depths. Local people have added a claim that the priests (sounding like Laurel and Hardy) found a random, sickly woman whose features were disfigured by her suffering and passed her off as the unfortunate Lily. So Ralph was fooled, the fake Lily died, and the two villainous priests could breathe a sigh of relief.

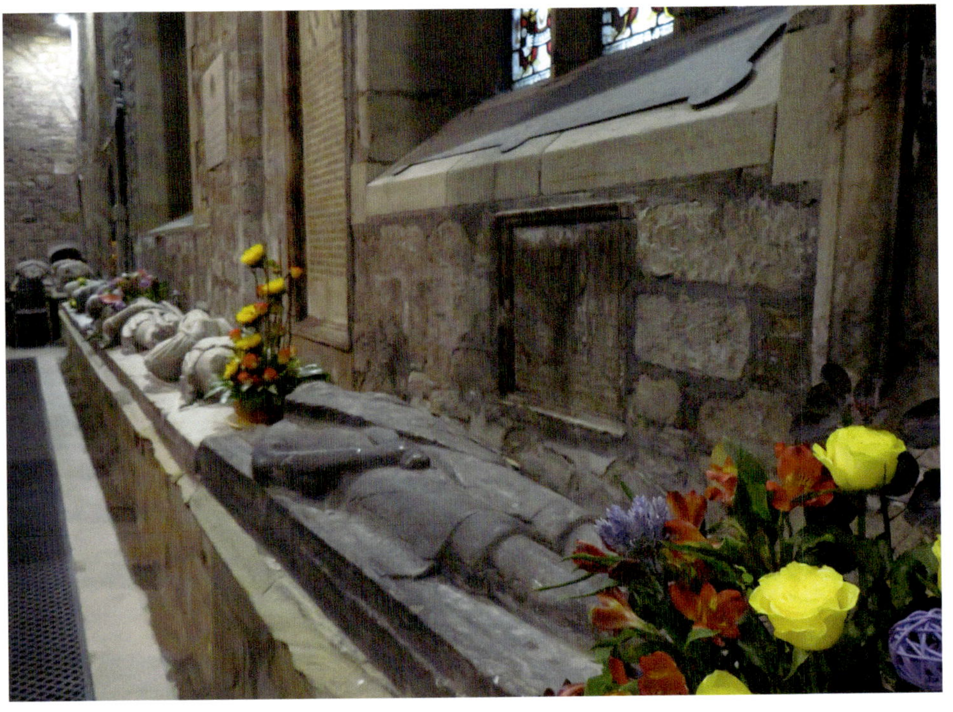

This collection of effigies in the church of St Mary and St Cuthbert's in Chester-le-Street supposedly includes Ralph Neville, husband of sad Lily. However, it has been suggested that many of the fourteen effigies donated by John Lumley in 1595 may not all be Lumleys.

In reality there is no record of Lady Lily at all. She sounds suspiciously like a late eighteenth-century Victorian creation designed to Gothicise Lumley Castle – as if it needed any Gothicisation! Ralph Lumley's second wife was a Neville, and one of the family who owned Raby Castle at the time.

From Chester-le-Street follow the busy A167 to Durham City which has lots and lots of ghosts. Start by wandering along the banks of the Wear to the thirteenth-century Crook Hall which is haunted by a White Lady said to be the niece of the volatile Cuthbert Billingham, who inherited in 1615. Rumour has it that he murdered her in one of his rages by pushing her downstairs. Thus, a woman with ivory skin and a long white gown is sometimes seen by visitors, a flickering and tormented figure adding to the tourist appeal of the ancient building.

Follow the riverside to Framwellgate Bridge where a ghostly figure known as Simple Jimmy is said to roam. Jimmy lived during the late eighteenth century. He was, apparently, a man with a childlike mentality. He spent his days wandering the streets, doing odd jobs to earn a bob or two. He had a particular fondness for the market on Framwellgate Bridge, where he would sit for hours. He would often play pranks and playfully push locals. It is claimed that visitors have reported feeling uneasy near Framwellgate Bridge, or in the shadowy alleyways. Some felt they were being followed by something, or someone, and without warning getting gently shoved. Personally, I can assert that I have felt haunted only by traffic wardens.

Cross over Framwellgate Bridge into the marketplace, and turn left down to Elvet Bridge for an encounter with Jimmy Allen the Piper. Born into a gypsy family in Northumberland in the 1720s he did time in the army and prison – and escaped from both. He became famous as a player of the smallpipes. Then in 1803 he was arrested for horse stealing and sentenced to transportation. Held in the house of correction beneath Elvet Bridge, he was in his early seventies and his health was deteriorating. King George III was petitioned to grant a pardon. It arrived four days too late because Allen had died on 13 November 1810. The entrance to the old house of correction is still visible. If you stand there at closing time you may hear the eerie sound of smallpipes.

Continue on to the fifteenth-century Dun Cow in Old Elvet which is claimed to be haunted by the ghost of Mary Ann Cotton. A string of twenty-six murders led to her execution at Durham County Gaol in 1873. There are claims that her spirit still continues to roam around the site of the old gaol. The Dun Cow was where the hangman would stay, William Calcraft in Mary's case. Perhaps her tormented spirit followed him back after her flawed hanging? Fervent drinkers and tired staff swear they have seen objects move by themselves, have heard footsteps in the corridor and even seen apparitions in the bar. The inn is supposed also to be haunted by a former landlord – no doubt driven to distraction, pestered by tourists constantly asking about Mary Ann Cotton.

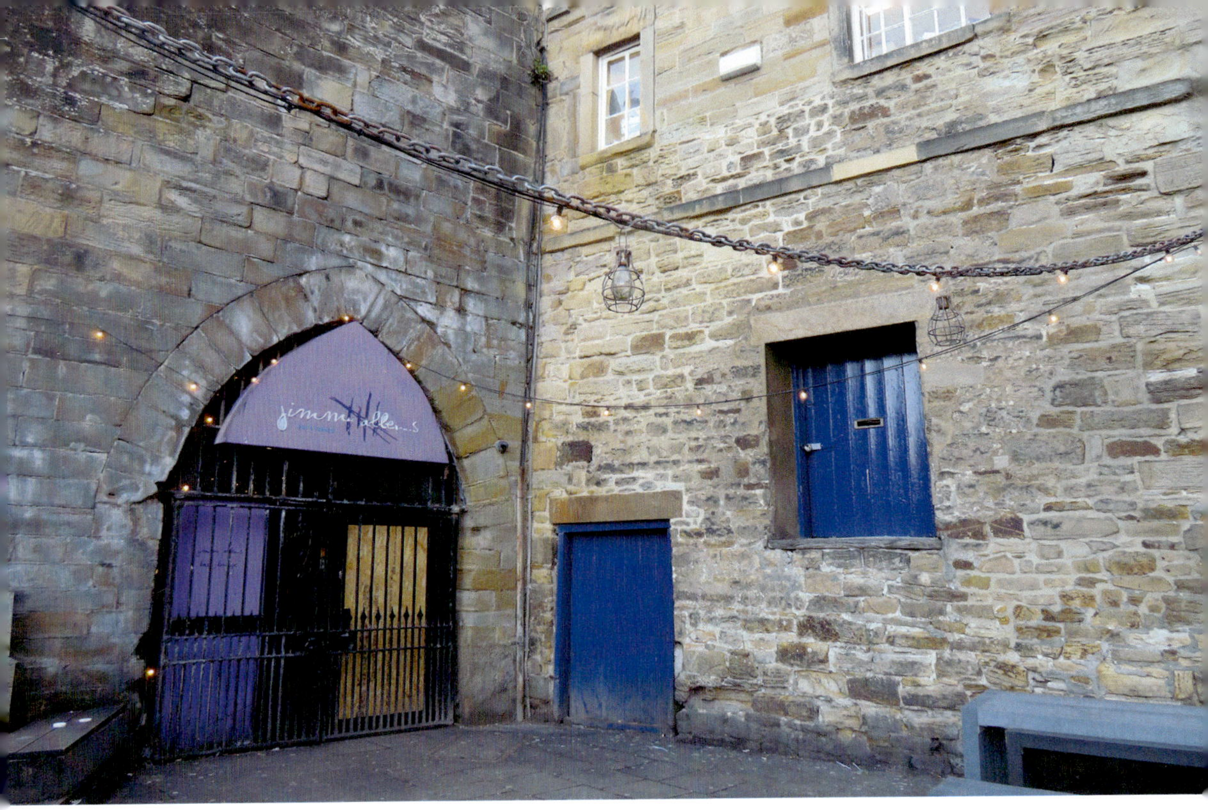

The entrance to the house of correction beneath Elvet Bridge where the piper Jimmy Allen died in 1810. You can still hear him playing, especially at night after a few drinks in the nearby hostelries.

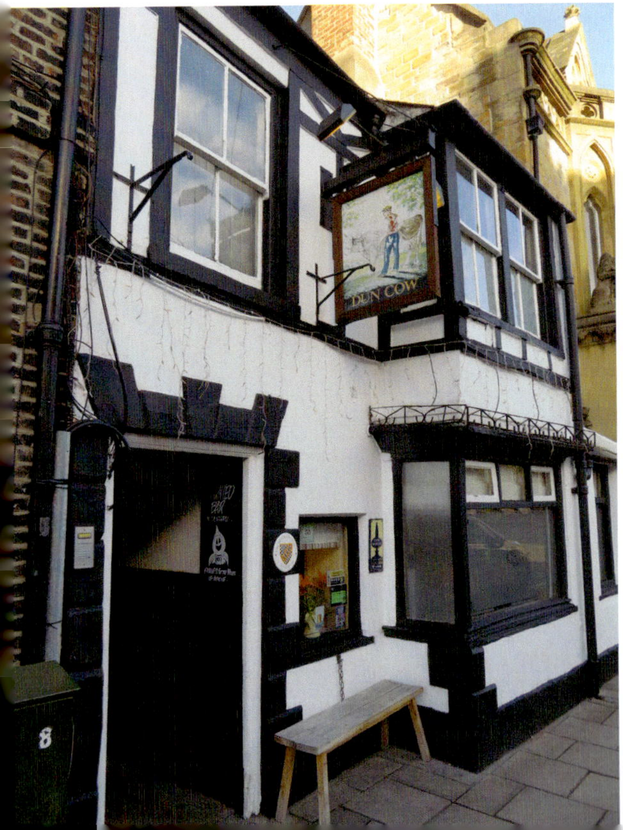

The Dun Cow in Old Elvet reflects, in its name, the legend of the founding of Durham. It also has two ghosts.

Re-cross Elvet Bridge and make your way up to Durham Castle. Whilst there, ponder the sad tale of the ghostly swot Frederick Copeman. One of the first students at the University, he lived in Room 21 at the top of the castle. Very nervous on the day of the publishing of examination results, Frederick woke early to check the board on Palace Green. His name wasn't on the list of students who had passed. Thinking he had failed, he returned to his room and was heard pacing around for hours, before taking his own life. Later it emerged that he had been awarded the highest honours possible but his name was hidden by another sheet of paper. To this day, it's said you can still hear Frederick's ghost as he paces around his room in anguish.

If you manage to join a tour of the castle look out for the so-called black staircase where you may encounter the Grey Lady. She is Isabella, the wife of Bishop William Van Mildert (1765–1836), who fell down the stairs, breaking her neck. She is also seen in the Norman Gallery, but only from the knees up due to the change in floor level. In fact, Van Mildert's wife was Jane Douglas and there is no evidence that she fell downstairs to her death, or was ever legless.

Of course, you and I might suggest that these stories sound suspiciously as if they might have been invented by senior Castle student residents to terrify nervous freshers!

Durham Castle was the Bishop's Palace until 1832. It has been university student accommodation since 1837, which may offer a clue as to the origin of two ghost stories.

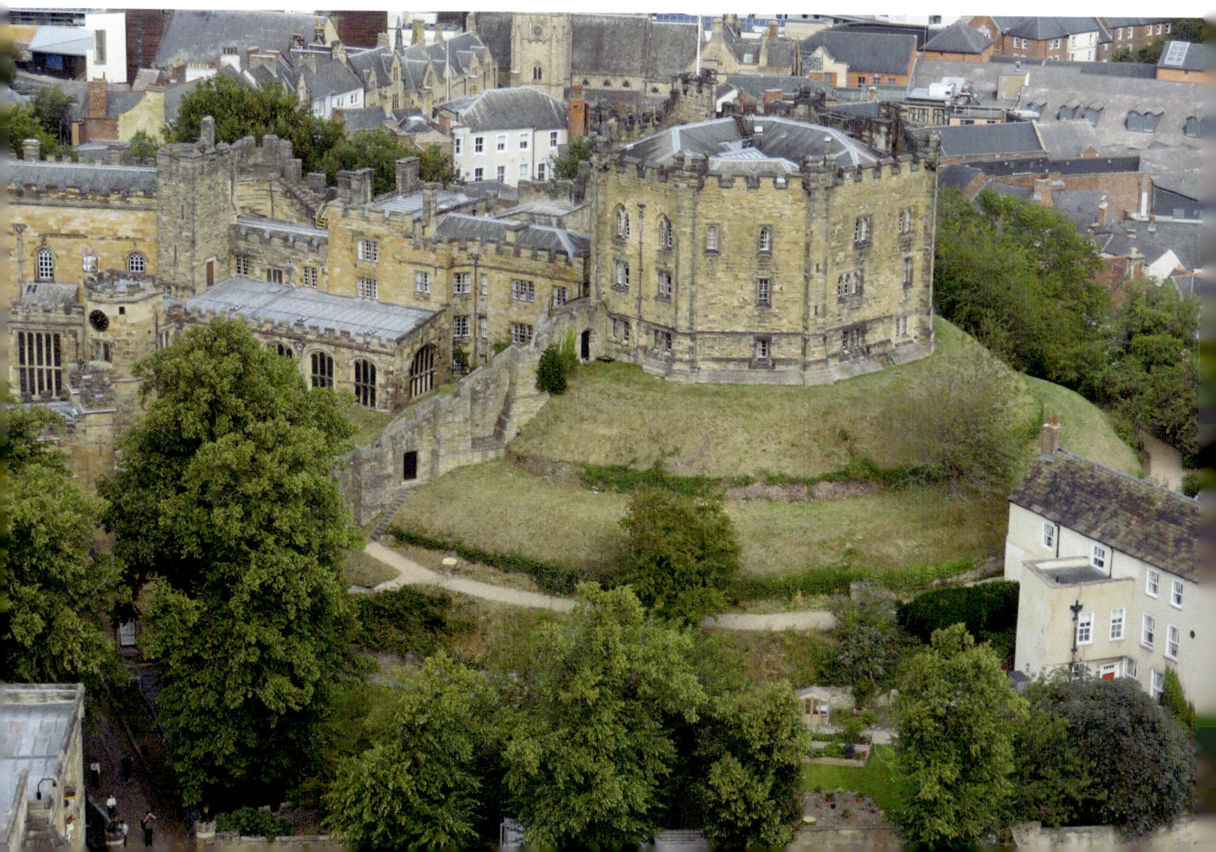

From Durham you could make excursions to pursue more apparitions. It is worth remembering that remark by Surtees that 'every castle, tower, or manor-house, has its visionary inhabitants', and such is true of so many of the great houses of County Durham. Distressed ladies in floaty dresses drifting through the rooms of great halls are common. Gothic novels often feature female ghosts trapped in their homes due to tragic events. The Victorians were much taken by ghosts. By 1887, when Mary Louise Molesworth wrote *The Story of the Rippling Train*, her character Mrs Snowdon was bemoaning ghosts' prevalence. 'One hears nothing else nowadays,' she said. No doubt flickering gas lighting and the carbon monoxide it emitted will have helped.

Just off the Lanchester road near Burnhope is Langley Hall. Inevitably it has a ghost. One of the owners was in financial difficulties and decided to marry a young woman to get her dowry. After the first night she fled in a carriage to return to her father. The husband gave chase, beheaded the coachman and killed his bride, before driving the coach into the marsh by Esh. It is this phantom coach that is said to be seen. In *Notes on the Folk-lore of the Northern Counties of England and the Borders* William Henderson says: 'Night after night … when it is sufficiently dark, the Headless (sic) Coach whirls along the rough approach to Langley Hall, near Durham, drawn by black and fiery steeds.' The ruins can still be seen but are heavily overgrown.

Sixteenth-century Langley Hall is now in a ruinous condition. The quiet road is haunted by a phantom carriage, a headless driver and a murdered bride.

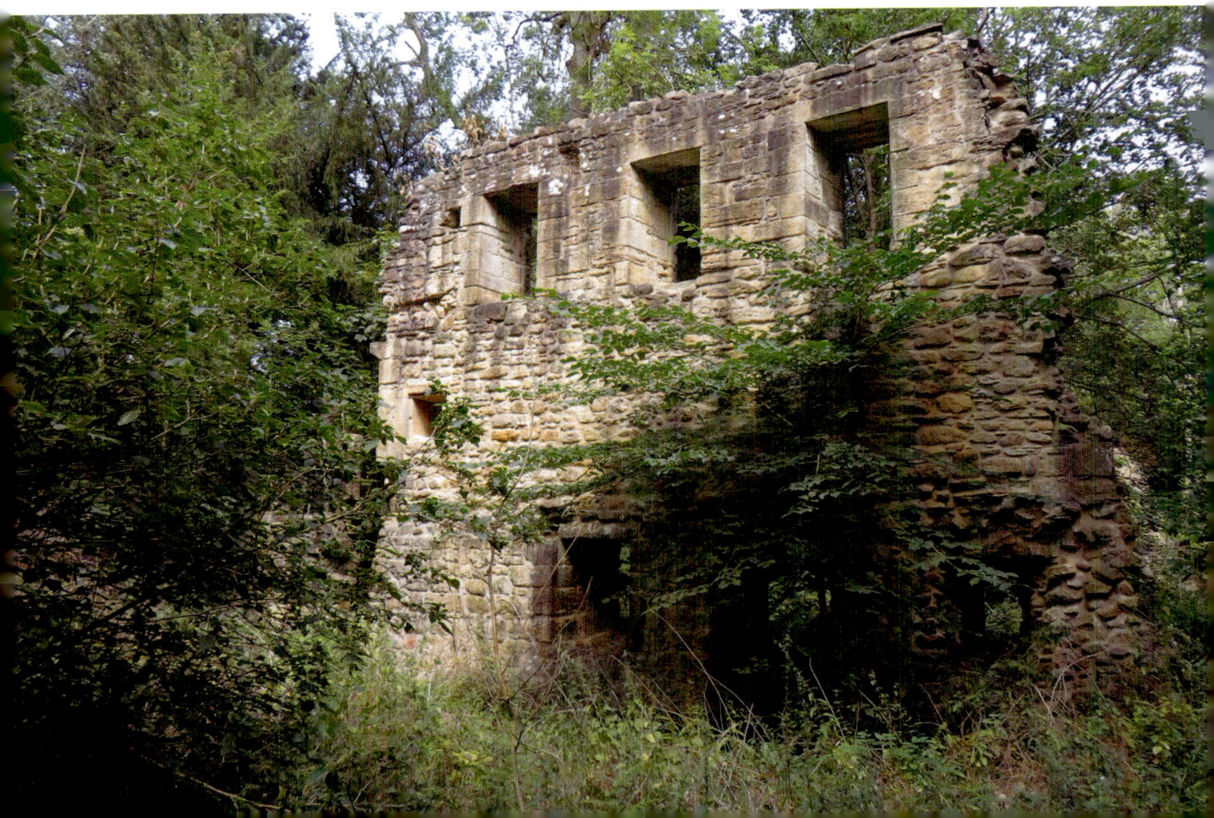

South of Chester-le-Street is Sedgefield, once the Parliamentary seat of Tony Blair. It is very near to Hardwick Hall which is haunted by a young girl who occasionally sits on beds, which makes a change from floating grey ladies. Sedgefield's fourteenth-century church, St Edmunds, and Ceddesfeld Hall overlook the village green. The hall was built by the brothers, Samuel and Shute Barrington. The former was an admiral and the latter was a Bishop of Durham. It was built for their nephew, George Barrington, who was the rector in the 1790s. Nevertheless, the ghost associated with the old rectory still haunts the site and was spiritual in more senses than one.

The story dates from 1747, when Revd John Gamage was rector. In the second week of December, he died, and left a problem. At that time the parson collected an annual tithe from parishioners. The tithes had to be paid on 20 December and provided an income for the clergyman. If the parish lacked a clergyman the money would go to the bishopric of Durham. Thus, his family faced the prospect of destitution. The redoubtable Mrs Gamage decided to preserve the body with salt until the crucial date. Only on the day after the tithes had all been paid, did she summon the doctor, who pronounced the parson dead.

However, another version has it that the widow kept her husband's body fresh by soaking him in brandy and propped him up in the window so that the tithe payers could see him and assume that all was well. You would have thought that the parson would have been pleased with his dexterous wife. But because he had not had a proper Christian burial, the parson's soul could not enter Heaven, so the stranded spirit returned to vex the village. Apparently, the rectory became haunted with all sorts of disturbances thus 'making the night hideous' according to Brockie.

In 1792 the old rectory burnt down. However, the Pickled Parson continued his haunting. Indeed, it is asserted by locals that there used to be a tunnel between the church and the rectory and that he walks the tunnel and is liable to appear at any time. This all adds to that bright tapestry of English folklore, helps to generate tourist income, and encourages visitors to the hotel the Pickled Parson and the village centre.

From Sedgefield meander on towards Darlington. Built in 1970, the Town Hall now stands on the site of the old Bishop's Palace. During the War of Three Kingdoms a certain Lady Jarrett was living at the palace. One version of the story is that she was murdered by her footman but the general consensus is that it was a roaming band of Cromwellian Roundheads who chased her. Unable to remove a valuable ring, they cut off her arm with one slash of a sword, gathered up whatever else they could find of value and fled. She staggered outside and reached an arch before collapsing leaving a bloody handprint.

It was her ghost, the Grey Lady (inevitably), which came to be seen in the palace. Apparently bloodstains and the bloody handprint remained into the twentieth century and could not be removed, even with a touch of Vim. It was claimed that eerie footfalls and the sound of her rustling silk dress were heard.

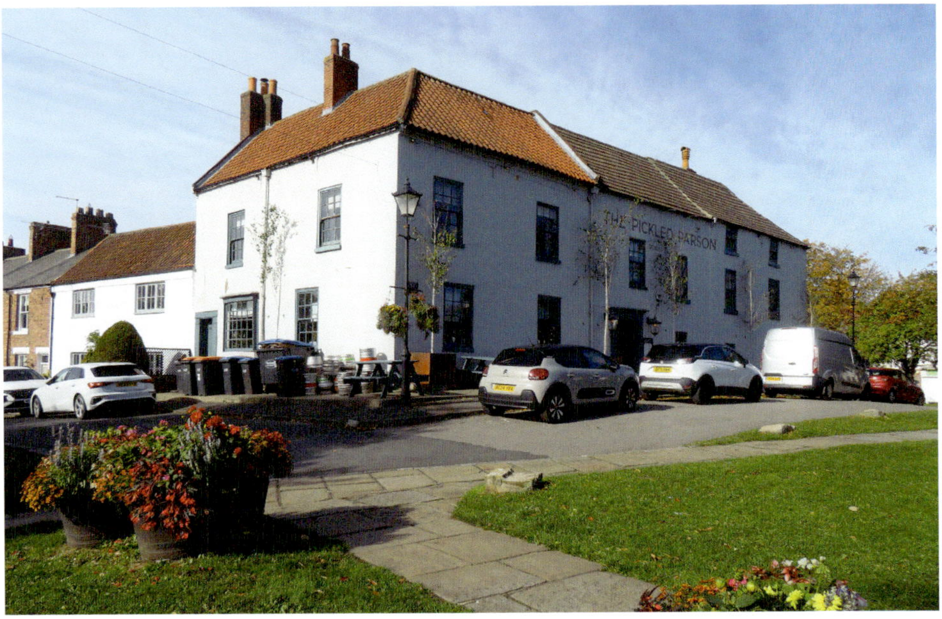

The uniquely named Pickled Parson in Sedgefield refers to the folk tale of the preserved clergyman.

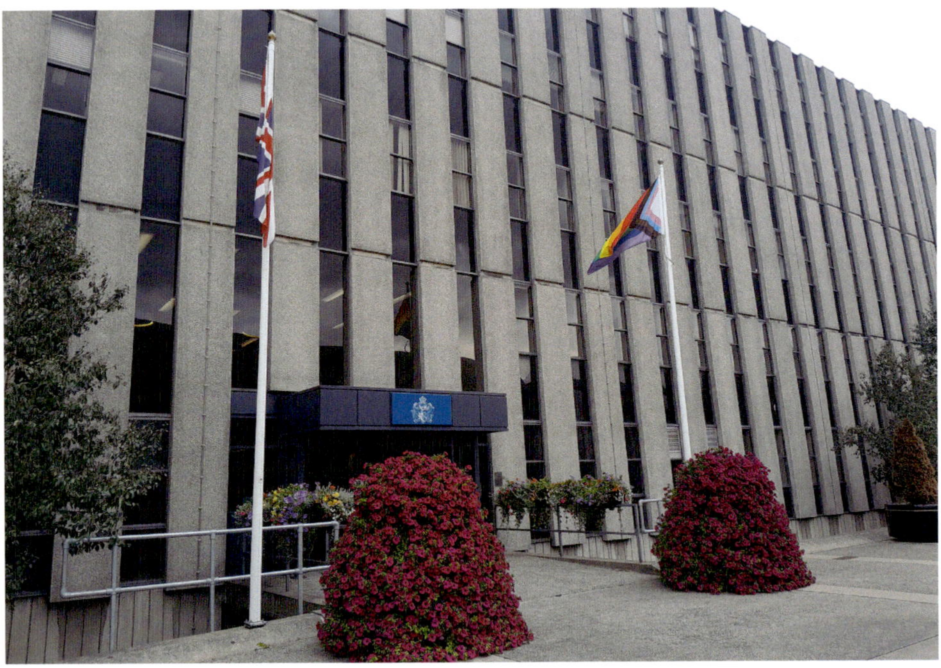

Darlington Town Hall, with its brutalist exterior, might seem an unlikely place to be haunted. The council employees may be unaware of the wild-eyed, one-armed woman who lurks within.

Even her breath could be felt. Furthermore, despite a blameless reputation in life, the ghost became malevolent. In 1854, she was described by the historian W. Hylton Dyer Longstaffe as 'a Robin Goodfellow', a term for a mischievous sprite renowned for playing tricks on unwary passers-by. When in 1703 the palace was turned into a workhouse, the paupers are claimed to have reported many instances of seeing her. Servants often had their bedclothes pulled from them. The cook was forever hearing a tune played on the copper. Lady Jarrett was said to have attended every birth and death in the workhouse. On one occasion a workhouse inmate was ill, so she made a cup of coffee to ease their suffering.

In 1870 a builder called Richard Luck bought the palace. Demolition began immediately because Luck wanted the land to build a residential square. During the demolition he was said to have found a bloody handprint left perfectly intact. But what was more disturbing was his close encounter with the lady:

> The end room was where Lady Jarrett was murdered and the bloodstains which could not be washed off were there. I was soon very much engaged in my work when I heard footsteps coming out of this room and I could feel it was her Ladyship. I could hear the rustle of her silk dress and she came close until I could feel her breath and her dress as she stooped over my shoulder to see what I was doing. I stood it for a very short while and then bolted along the corridor as hard as I could go.

The one-armed ghost was even seen wandering, disconcertingly, among shoppers in the town centre. Her last recorded appearance was in 1938.

There is no evidence of a Lady Jarrett but there was a Lady Gerard who was the daughter of the Prince Bishop of Durham, John Cosin. However, while Cosin held the post from 1660 to 1672 the soldiers are said to have killed Lady Gerard between 1642 and 1651. The bishop before Cosin never married and had no daughters. Cosin's daughter married Gilbert Gerard, Constable of Billingham, but she didn't die until 1680. So, if a woman did die at the Darlington Prince Bishop's Palace due to some violent Civil War soldiers, she was no relation to Cosin or Gerard. Does it really matter though? It's such a good story.

The arch is said to have been moved to the South Park in 1938. If it was, it was demolished in 2011. The site of the palace is now where the Town Hall stands. It is claimed that an underground tunnel leads to St Cuthbert's Church and that the errant spectre has taken up residence in it. Others have reported seeing her glide across the River Skerne and in the South Park. I never got beyond the nice coffee shop though. Other witnesses have testified that her death did not remove her spirit from the old Bishop's Palace where she now, presumably, flutters between filing cabinets and photocopiers.

So on towards Barnard Castle, via Raby Castle the home of the incorrigible Vanes. Christopher Vane, 1st Baron Barnard, was a quiet man who liked an easy life but married Lady Elizabeth Holles who had an 'ungovernable temper'.

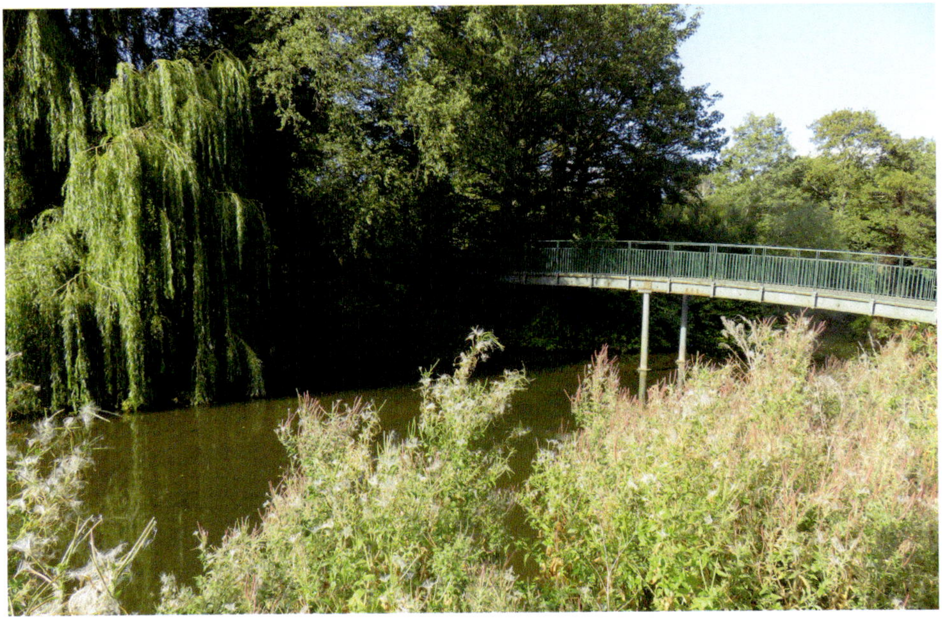

The lovely and well-manicured South Park in Darlington is haunted by the peripatetic Lady Gerrard, aka Jarrett, who floats across the Skerne. There's a nice coffee shop as well.

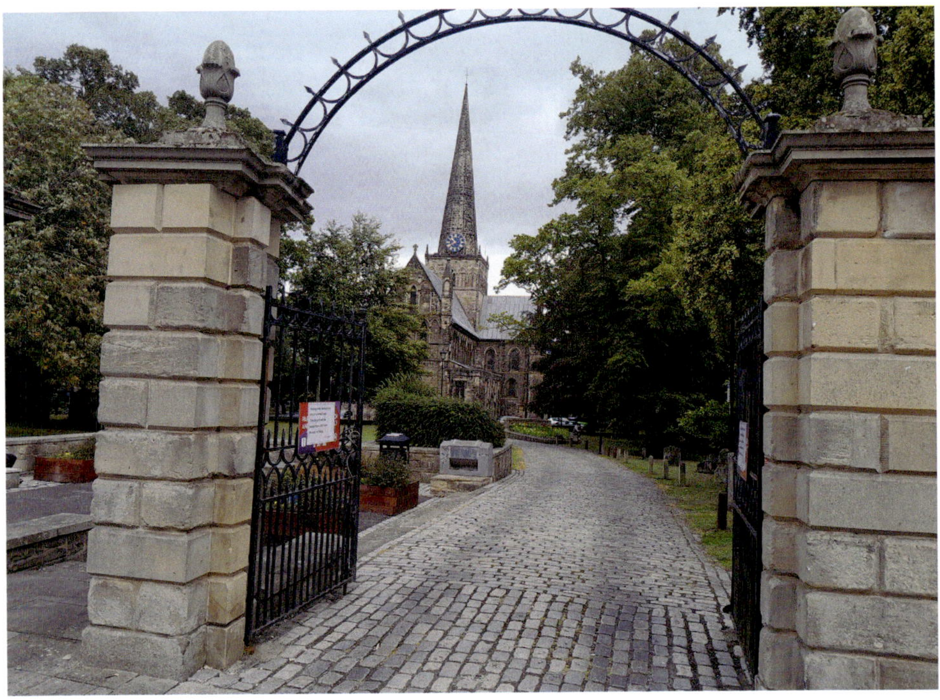

St Cuthbert's in Darlington is claimed to be linked to the former Bishop's Palace, now town hall, by a tunnel through which the ghost of Lady Jarrett aka Gerrard commutes.

In 1714, their eldest son Gilbert announced his intention to marry Mary, the daughter of Guildford MP Morgan Randyll who was very rich but a commoner. Christopher and Elizabeth were furious and in protest against the marriage set about destroying his inheritance. Christopher paid £50 to employ 200 workmen.

The castle was stripped of its lead, glass, doors and furniture in days, and the floors were all pulled up. The woodlands were cut down and many of the famous deer were slaughtered. Household goods were sold off for a pittance, and what remained ended on an enormous bonfire. Gilbert and Mary took Christopher and Elizabeth to court and they were ordered to cease the destruction. Rebuilding, replanting and refurnishing began. Despite all this, Gilbert and Mary had a happy marriage.

But the awful Elizabeth continued to torment her neighbours and became known locally as 'the Old Hell Cat'. She haunts the battlements of Raby Castle to this very day, pacing furiously back and forth, knitting with red-hot needles. I've never seen her but that doesn't mean she isn't there.

Our last stop is Barnard Castle – once an unlikely venue for Covid eye tests! Close by, near the rendezvous of Greta and Tees at Dairy Bridge, stands

The Dairy Bridge near Mortham Tower spans the noisy River Greta just before it joins the Tees. This area was popular with artists such as Turner and Cotman, as well as Sir Walter Scott, a frequent visitor to Rokeby Hall which was the setting for his epic poem *Rokeby*.

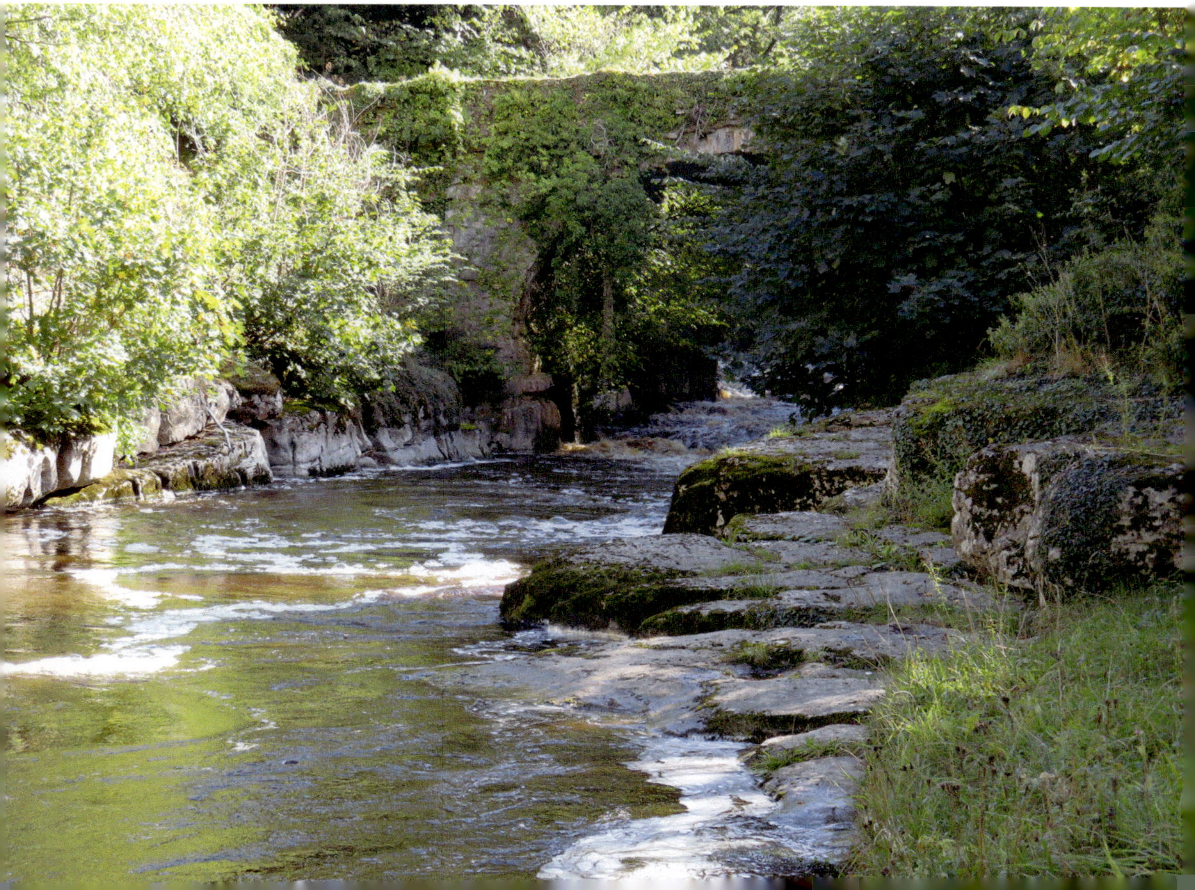

Mortham Tower which is a splendid example of a fortified courtyard house built after an earlier building was destroyed by Scottish raiders in 1343. The estate was originally the seat of the Rokeby family. While the essentials of the original house still exist, it was extended and altered in the 18th Century. Mortham Tower has a ghost, of course. She is a Rokeby lady who was murdered by either a relative or robbers. In the first volume of *Memoirs of the Life of Sir Walter Scott: In Three Volumes*, John G. Lockhart says:

> ...she certainly became a ghost and under the very poetic *nom de guerre* of Mortham Dobby, she appeared dressed as a fine lady with a piece of white silk trailing behind her, without a head indeed though no tradition states how she lost so material a member, but with many of its advantages for she had long hair on her shoulders and eyes nose and mouth in her breast. The parson once by talking Latin to her, confined her under the bridge that crosses the Greta at my dairy, but the arch being destroyed by floods in 1771 became incapable of containing a ghost any longer...I often heard of her in my early youth from a Sibyl who lived in the park to the age of 105, but since her death I believe the history has become obsolete.

If in doubt, ask a neighbourhood Sibyl. They crop up a lot in folk tales.

5
Icons and Monuments

As well as ghosts, the county is also rich in statues, monuments, castles and bridges. Here we examine some of the folk tales attached to them.

The greatest architectural icon of County Durham must be Penshaw Monument. Penshaw Hill is a prominent 136-metre (446-ft) knoll formed by the erosion of an escarpment of the Durham Magnesian Limestone Plateau. What appear to be the remains of Iron Age triple ramparts have been identified. It is very much associated with the Lambton Worm. The famous folk song by C. M. Leumane in 1867 describes the worm wrapping itself 'ten times roond Pensha Hill'. As well as the worm connection, there are fairy folk haunting the Hill as well. The Penshaw fairies and the Lambton Worm are encountered elsewhere.

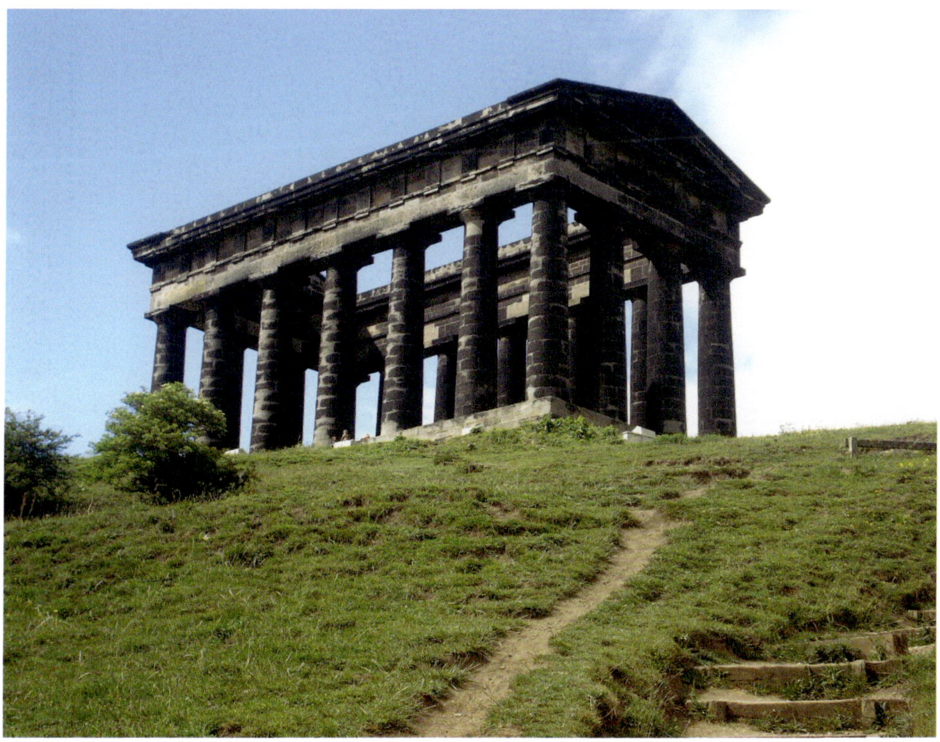

The Penshaw Monument as seen from the parking area to the south. The iconic Greek-style memorial was built between 1844 and 1845. It is not a folly, as is so often claimed. It is in the care of the National Trust who restored it from near collapse. Occasionally, the stairs in one of the columns are opened to the public and there are splendid panoramic views.

Strictly speaking, the Earl of Durham's monument was built between 1844 and 1845 to commemorate John Lambton, 1st Earl of Durham (1792–1840), author of the 'Durham Report on the Future Governance of Canada' regarded as the foundation document of the British Commonwealth of Nations. The monument has been in the care of the National Trust since 1939. It is based on the Temple of Hephaestus in Athens, albeit half the size with eighteen columns. One column contains a spiral staircase leading to a walkway. Since 2011, the National Trust has supervised tours, and even abseiling. It was substantially restored in 1979. There is a local myth that it is incomplete and that the statue of the man on horseback in Durham was intended to be on the top of it. In fact, it is complete; it was designed to be roofless. The 'man' is the Marquess of Londonderry, not the 1st Earl of Durham, so why would he be on the top of a memorial to one of his greatest business rivals? The Marquess did actually provide the stone from his quarry.

The most intriguing story is that Penshaw Monument arose from the gratitude of the tenantry of the Earl of Durham for his lowering of their rents after peace came in 1815 when the price of corn plummeted. However, the Earl was aghast at the amount of money that his tenants had been able to subscribe for this purpose, so he then increased their rents. Now this is untrue. But not that far away, at Alnwick, tenant farmers actually did that on behalf of their landlord, the 2nd

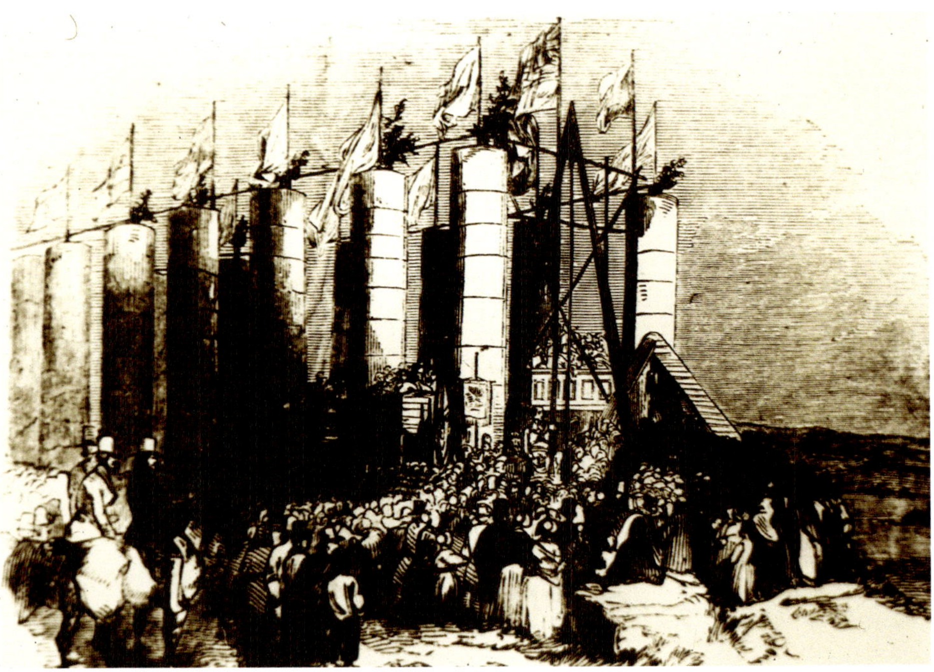

It is claimed that the Lambton tenants, estate and colliery workers donated their pennies towards the building of the famous monument. This is just another local folk tale about the monument.

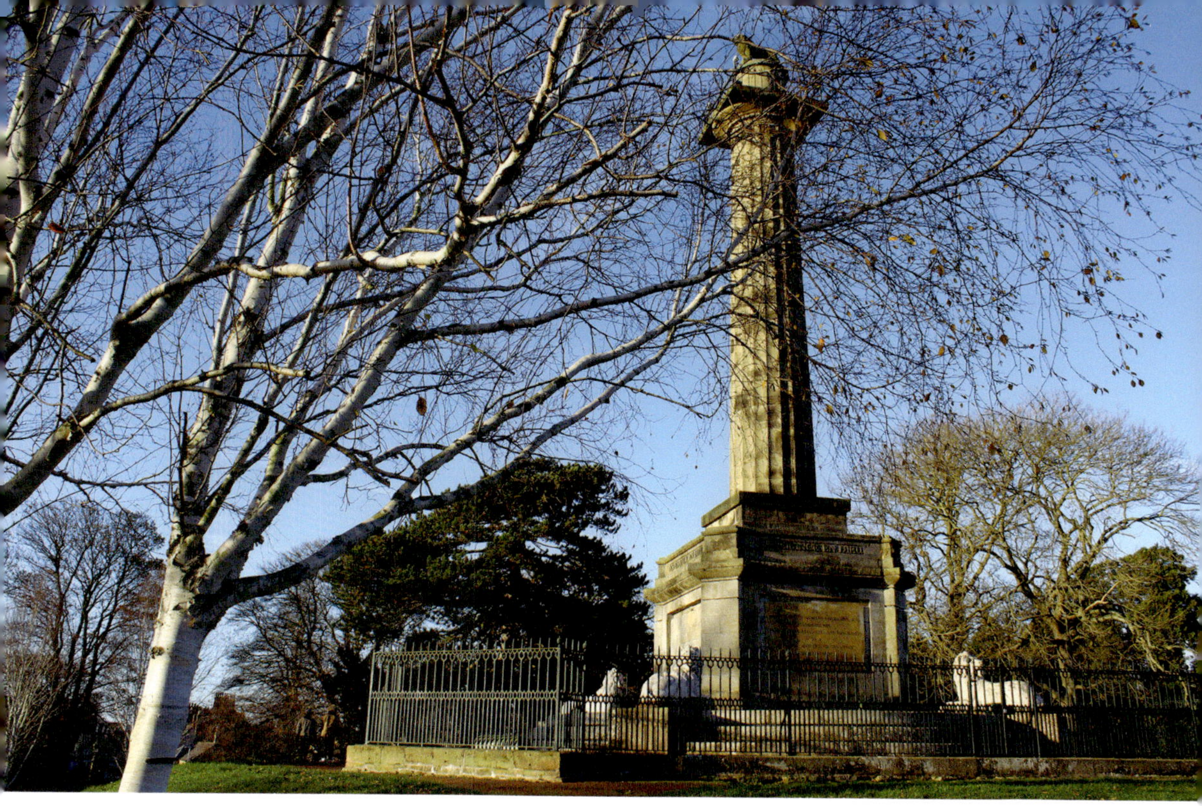

The imposing Tenantry Column in Alnwick about which a folk tale similar to that about the Penshaw Monument has been created, although the Alnwick version is partly true.

Duke of Northumberland, when the famous Tenantry Column, sometimes called the Farmers' Folly, was erected. The Duke did not then raise the rents, however, although there is a persistent local myth that he did. This is an example of the transmission of urban myths. The £6,000 needed for Penshaw Monument was actually raised by subscription from businessmen and landowners.

The process of transferring a good story from one location to another is not uncommon. A classic example is the story of the bells of Blanchland Abbey.

Blanchland is a picture-perfect village on the edge of the moorland fells of the North Pennines. It was created in the eighteenth century from the ruins of a monastery. The abbey was founded in 1165 by Premonstratensian canons who wore white habits (perhaps the origin of the name 'Blanche-land'?). Never very wealthy, it lingered on until 1539 when it was dissolved. The nave was demolished but many monastic buildings survived. The Abbot's lodging became a manor house and is the Lord Crewe Arms Hotel today. The gatehouse and cottages, originally the outer court of the monastery, form a village square. Hence the sense of Blanchland being a planned village. In 1704, the estate was purchased by Lord Crewe, the Bishop of Durham. On his death in 1721, it was left to the Lord Crewe Charity Trust. I've included it here because of the Crewe connection even though the village is actually in Northumberland.

The monks chose a good location. It was isolated and hidden from predators. The Anglo-Scottish border was, for centuries, troubled by intermittent raiding by

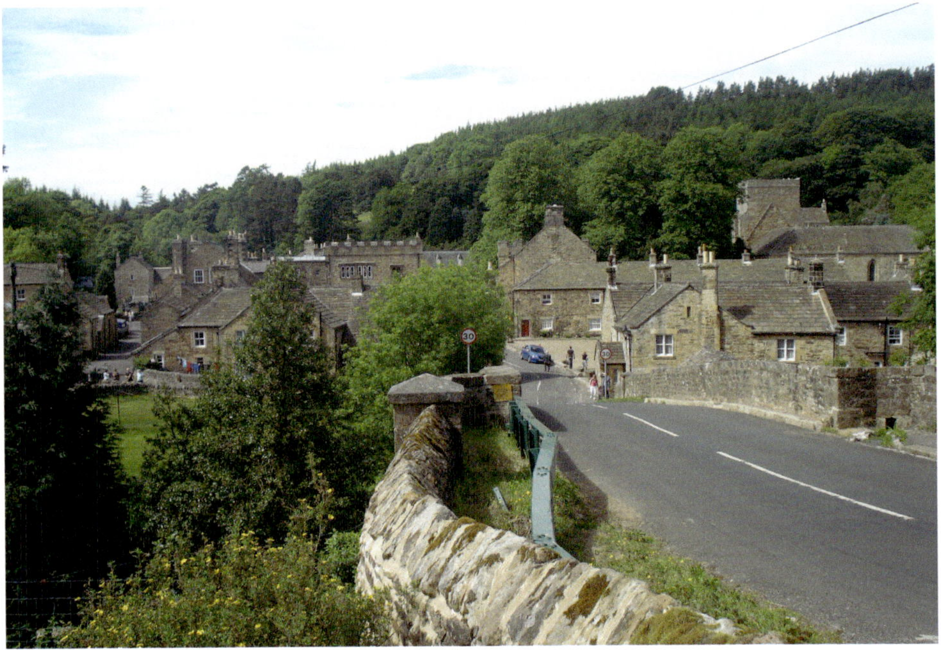

The lovely village of Blanchland seen from the bridge over the Derwent. It is actually in Northumberland but there is a very good reason for including it in this collection.

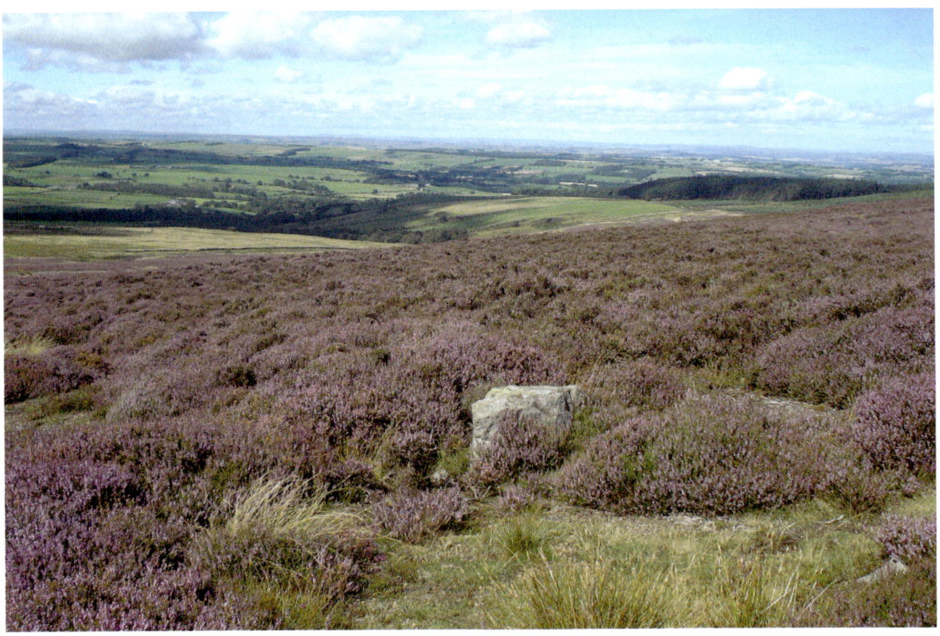

Heathery Blanchland Moor looking north towards Hexhamshire. The route by which Scottish raiders would come to loot, burn and shoplift in the very welcoming store and post office.

the so-called border reivers interrupted occasionally by formal warfare. In these circumstances the settlements of holy men like the Blanchland monks were by no means immune and were full of rich pickings. However, although they knew of the monastery, the border raiders could never find it because it was so well hidden in the hill folds and dense woodland. Then one day a Scottish raiding party came riding over the moors. Miraculously, as they approached the abbey, a dense mist fell so they could see only a few yards ahead. They lost their way and were observed by a monastic watcher to pass by cursing the fog and the dank, slippery terrain. At that point the monk ran to tell the abbot that the community was safe. They retrieved hidden valuables and rang the bells to celebrate their unscathed survival. That was a mistake. The blundering Scots heard the sound, turned their ponies and trotted back across the moorland. Bursting through the gates they rushed into the church, killed the abbot and monks and seized their treasures. Then they set fire to the buildings, and soon Blanchland was no more than smouldering ruins. So not quite a happy ending!

What are we to make of this? First of all, there is no evidence for it. There was a great increase in border warfare and reiving from the late thirteenth century when Edward I began to interfere seriously in the matter of succession to the throne of Scotland. A visit by the king could be even worse. As a result of the visit by Edward III and his army in 1327, the abbey was depleted of its resources and the monks appealed to the king later for assistance to help restore their fortunes. There is some placename 'evidence' because to the south of Blanchland on the Durham side of the Derwent there is a point called Dead Friar's Hill which is where, supposedly, the raiders heard the bells. However, the name could have been added to embellish the story.

There is another version of this story around the theme of lying low, saying nothing and avoiding trouble. This one tells of Henry VIII's commissioner coming to inspect Blanchland Abbey in 1535 before its dissolution. While the commissioner could not find his way in the mist, the canons had rung the abbey bells in celebration. The commissioner thanked them profusely for signalling their whereabouts! The only 'evidence' for this story is John Carr's interminable forty-verse *Ode to the Derwent*. Carr came from Muggleswick and was the son of a farmer who became a schoolmaster and classical scholar. However, his poem was written in 1732, 400 years later, on the basis of no obvious source apart from a mysterious 'black chronicle', and at a time when medievalism was being rediscovered and often manufactured, as with *The Bard of Ossian* by James Macpherson in the 1760s.

I much prefer the one about the Scottish raiders lost in the mist. The lost inquisitor version is more like a health and safety inspector being delayed because of sat nav problems.

What is intriguing is that here is another example of the apparent duplication of a striking story involving Brinkburn Priory in Northumberland. As an extra, though, the fateful bell that lured the Scots through the mists is still, supposedly,

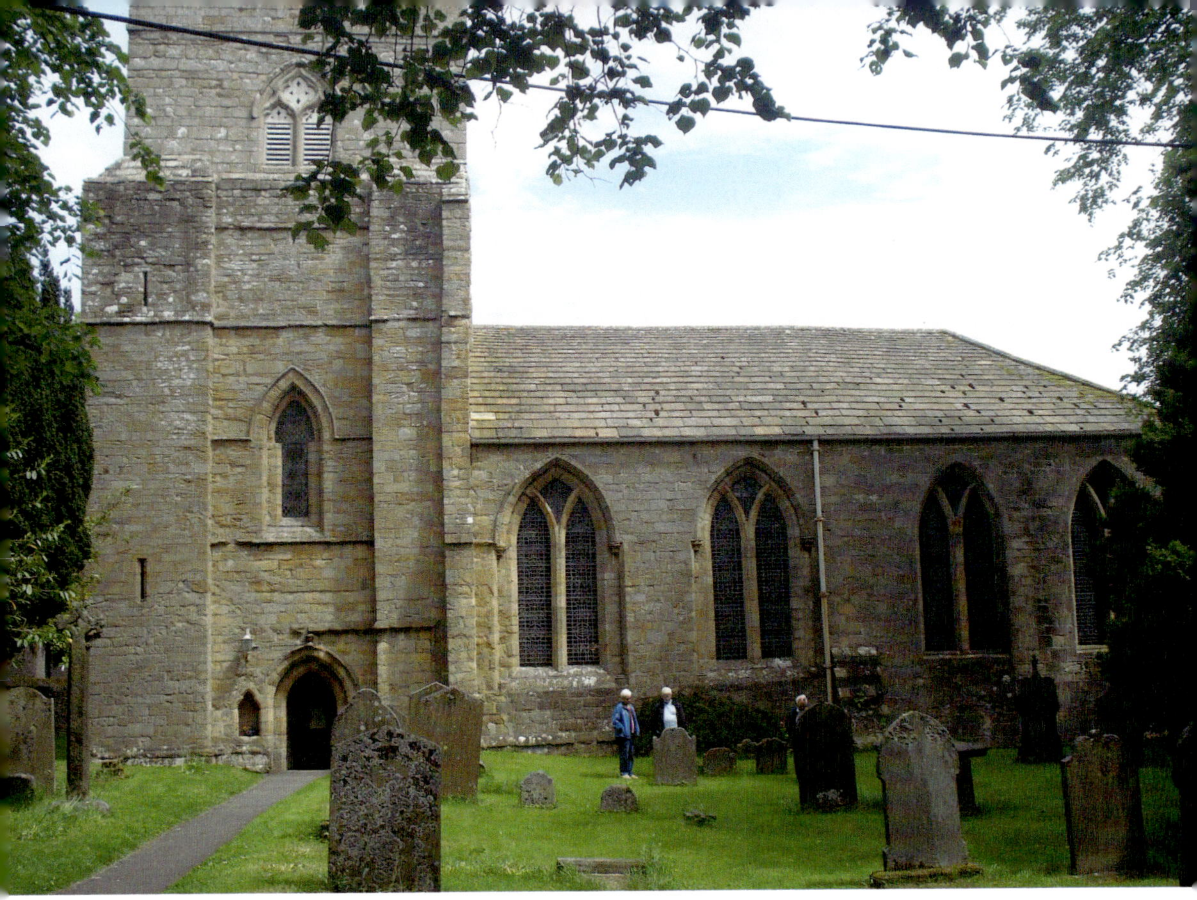

Blanchland Abbey was founded in 1165 by Walter de Bolbec. It was dissolved in 1539.

in the depths of the so-called Bell Pool, where it either rolled in during the conflagration, was hidden to protect a very expensive item, or was hurled in as a punishment of the bell.

In Durham city centre there are two statues. The lead statue of Neptune was given to the city in 1729 by the wealthy coal owner and landowner George Bowes. It was symbolic of a fantastic plan to provide Durham with a navigable link to the sea at a time of great speculation in infrastructural ventures. This was one of the schemes that never actually took off though, so Neptune was a little premature.

The other very prominent statue is a martial one of Charles William Vane Stewart, the 3rd Marquess of Londonderry, on horseback. The Marquess was a cavalryman during the Napoleonic Wars. His second wife was Lady Frances Anne, daughter and heiress of Sir Henry Vane-Tempest. Londonderry took the surname of Vane. He used his wife's wealth to acquire the Seaham Hall estate and to develop the coalfields in that area. The town and harbour of Seaham were largely his creation. When he died in 1854, his widow raised money to erect a grand statue. The Swiss-born Raffaelle Monti from Milan made the statue using plaster electroplated with copper. Monti went bankrupt, and the statue was confiscated to pay his debts, so the widow had to pay the debts to get it back.

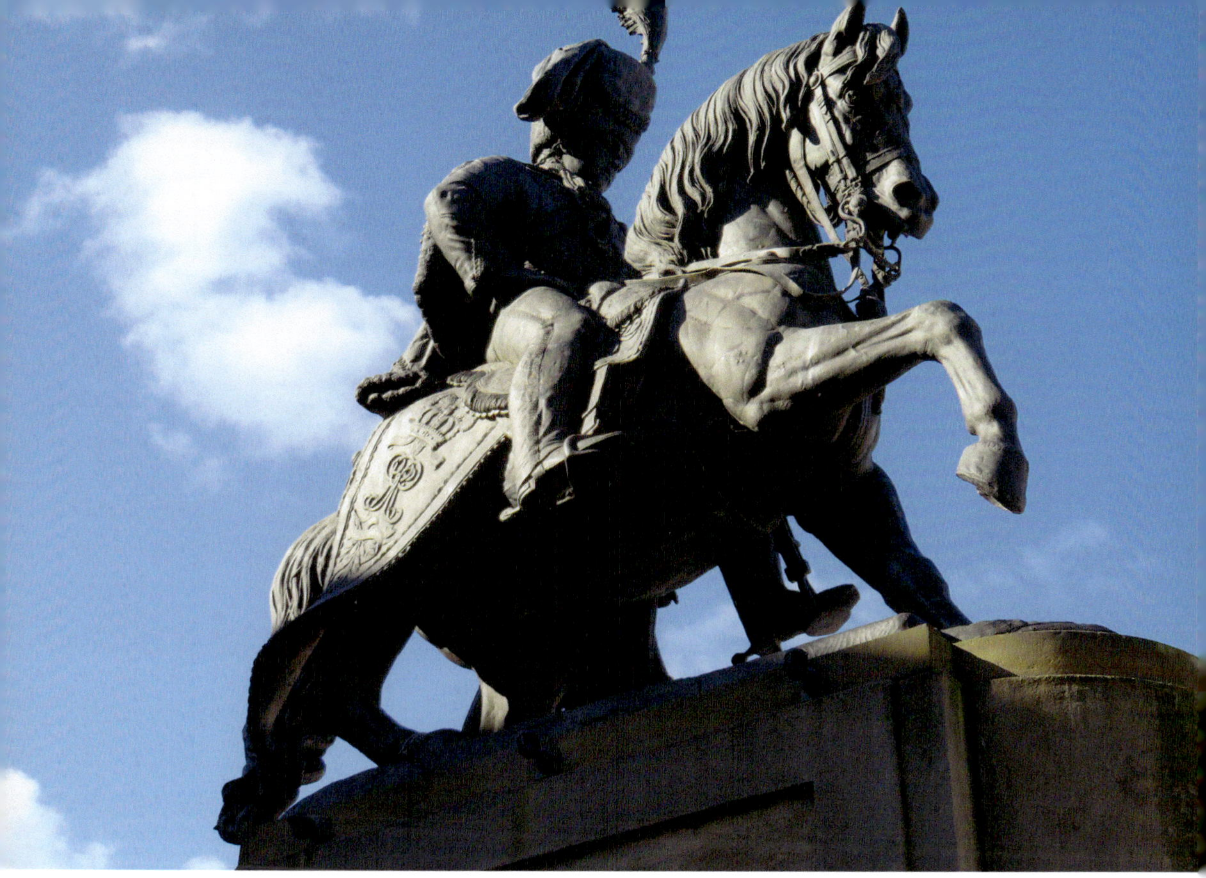

Monti's statue of the Marquess of Londonderry in Durham is one of two prominent statues in the market square. Both have very prominent rear ends which have been themselves a subject of controversy.

Local tradesmen opposed the idea because they claimed the statue could inhibit traffic. Ultimately, though, the Marquess took up his position in 1861, and thankfully so because it is such a striking feature of the city. However, a peculiar legend became associated with it.

It is said the sculptor was so taken by the quality of his work that when friends asked him if he was confident in the perfection of his creation, he said that he would kill himself if anyone found even the slightest flaw in it. He was a well-liked man but the more he boasted the more people were tempted to test his ideal of perfection, so people pored all over it, feeling it and peering into every feature. A servant of the horseman spent a day examining it and then finally admitted the artist had captured the likeness very well. On another occasion, a horse dealer came and felt every part of the equine body but was obliged to confess defeat. He said if a real horse had been turned to stone there could have been no more exact model. On a third occasion, a tailor swaggered up determined to find a fault. He inspected every fine detail, every stitch, every button but he too was forced to admit failure.

As a result, the boast of the sculptor was forgotten. Then one day a blind man came to town. He heard of the beauties of Durham. 'However,' the blind man was told, 'perhaps if you had eyesight you might have been able to detect the fault which has escaped everyone else!' Nevertheless, the beggar was determined to succeed where everyone else had failed. So next day he had his friends lift him onto the plinth. For hours he used his fingers to explore both horse and rider. It was only when the sun was setting that he asked his friends to lift him down again and to take him to the sculptor. Of course, the sculptor scorned the notion of a blind man being able to find any fault where so many others had failed. 'Sir,' said the beggar, 'what you have created is wonderful and so very near perfection, but there is a flaw.' 'There can be no flaw,' said the sculptor. 'How could a man without sight discern any imperfection?' And he and his fellows laughed at the very notion. Then the beggar said: 'The tongue. The horse has no tongue. Look again at your horse and you will find it has no tongue.'

So out they rushed across the square to the statue. And true enough they realised that a blind man had noticed what no others had been able to discover. The horse had no tongue. After that, the beggar went his way and was never seen again but the sculptor was so overcome that he killed himself that very night. And to this day the horse in Durham's market square has no tongue.

Sadly, the story is utter nonsense. The horse does have a tongue, and the well-respected sculptor Monti lived until 1881, much in demand and creating

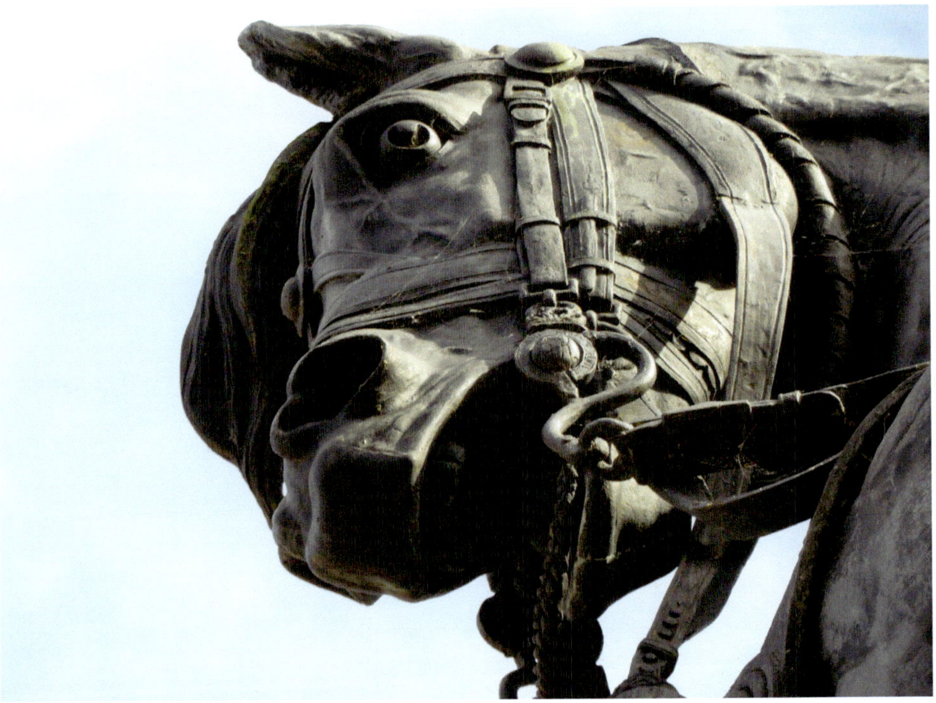

Monti's statue of the Marquess of Londonderry in Durham's market square. The horse has a tongue, in fact. Honestly! I haven't actually climbed up to feel it because there is usually a police presence. You can see it though.

many more statues – all with tongues. It is true, however, that both Neptune and the horse have very prominent bottoms in a very public setting and they have been the subject of controversy in their own right. But that is a different story.

One devastated creator dying by suicide because of a flaw in his pièce de résistance is bad enough, but two devastated creators dying by suicide is almost becoming a pattern! There is indeed another Monti-like story elsewhere in County Durham, but this one has to do with a bridge.

The Causey Arch near Stanley is the oldest surviving single-arch purpose-built railway bridge in the world. It carried an early wagonway for horse-drawn carts to transport coal. It was built in 1725–26 by stonemason Ralph Wood, funded by a monopolistic consortium of coal owners. When completed, it was the longest single-span bridge in the country with an arch span of 31 metres (102 feet). An inscription on a sundial, now gone, read 'Ra. Wood, mason, 1727'. Use of the arch declined when Tanfield Colliery was destroyed by fire in 1739. It was restored and reinforced in the 1980s when it was in imminent danger of collapsing.

The story is that after he built the bridge, Wood was so afraid that it would collapse that he killed himself in 1727. Another version has it that the first structure collapsed before it was finished, and that Wood was worried that the second arch would go the same way. His behaviour became more and more eccentric. Eventually he jumped from the bridge to his death into the gorge below even before the arch was completed. In some versions he realised that he had forgotten a keystone (but keystones are in position). In some versions he hangs himself from the bridge. All of the versions have one thing in common: there is no evidence at all for any of them. Unfortunately, there is nothing more known about the humble Ralph Wood himself.

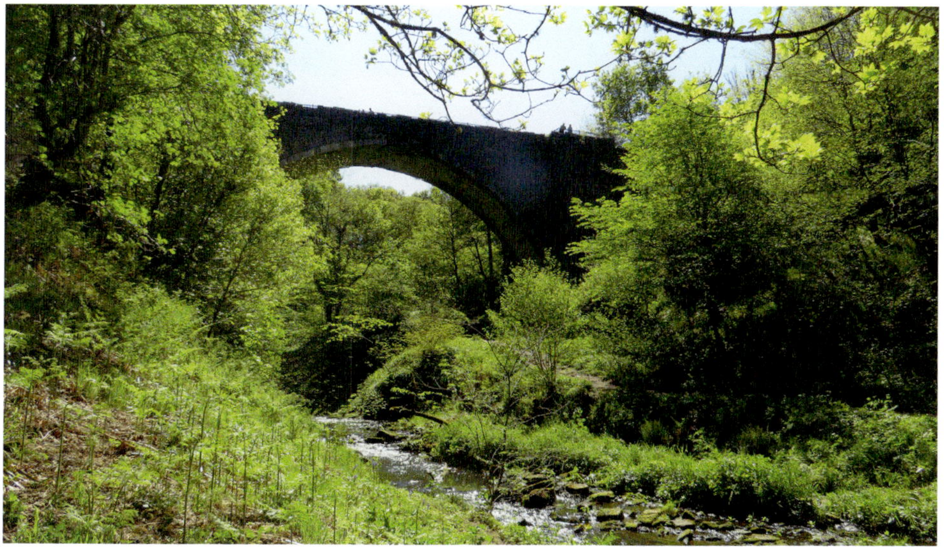

The Causey Arch Bridge is the world's oldest-surviving railway bridge.

6

Away with the Fairies!

Like Japanese knotweed, fairies are pernicious, persistent and almost impossible to eradicate. Forget the tiny, gossamer-winged Enid Blyton types because they aren't real.

Penshaw Hill was once a fairy hill where fairies gathered to bake bread and cakes and make butter. However, fairies can be vengeful creatures. According to *Legends and Superstitions of Durham* by William Brockie (1886):

> The fairies used to be heard patting their butter on the slope of Pensher Hill, when people were passing in the dark. A man once heard one of them say, 'mend that peel!'. Next day, going past again, he found a broken peel [a long-handled shovel] lying on the ground. So he took it up and mended it. The day after that, when going along the road with a cart, he saw a piece of bread lying on a stone at the root of the hedge, at the identical place, with nice-looking fresh butter spread upon it: but he durst neither eat it himself, nor give it to his horses. The consequence was that before he got to the top of the 'lonnin' both his horses fell down dead.

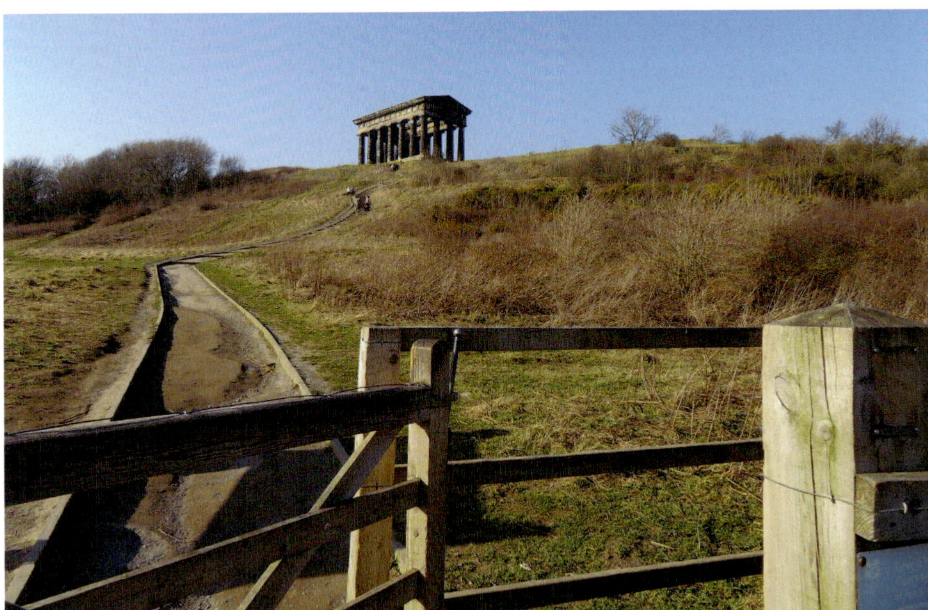

Penshaw Monument on Penshaw Hill, viewed from the south. 'Penshaw' actually means 'wooded hill', so the 'Hill' is duplicative.

So, I suggest that you beware of denying fairy gratitude. In fact, you might be wise to stay away from fairies altogether as evidenced by their behaviour at Stanhope and Middridge.

Near Middridge there was a popular meeting point for fairies. In summer nights they gathered in their hundreds and danced. Villagers sometimes visited the area to try and glimpse the fairy folk. If a young girl saw them, she would be favoured by marriage with her true love within the year whilst a stout young lad who witnessed them would be blessed by marriage to a very pretty girl.

However, according to Sidney Hartland, reporting an account by a local lady: 'Woe to those, however, who dared to come by twos or by threes, with inquisitive and curious eye, within the bounds of their domain; for if caught, or only the eye of a fairy fell upon them, ill was sure to betide them through life.'

Hartland's informant went on to tell him a sort of Tam O'Shanter tale about what could go wrong. Frederick Grice tells a version of this story as well, which he claims is based on an older version. I have spliced the two.

There was once a group of farm labourers and servants enjoying rather too much to drink. The last sheaf had been brought in, and conversation, inevitably, turned to the little people who lived upon the neighbouring hill in a deep quarry. Each participant had a tale to tell as had been received from their mothers and grandmothers. However, the younger men poured scorn on these accounts. At last, one of the loudest doubters, Willy by name, was dared to go the hill and ride around the quarry nine times then return. If he managed to do this he would have achieved something because by the time the ninth circuit was ended the angry fairies would be well alerted.

So off went Willy, full of the courage of drink. He was brave, even if boastful, and clever enough to take precautions. On his way he passed some rowan trees and cut up some bark into fragments because no evil spirit will ever pass a rowan tree or even a piece of rowan bark. Then he rode on. When he arrived, he cantered

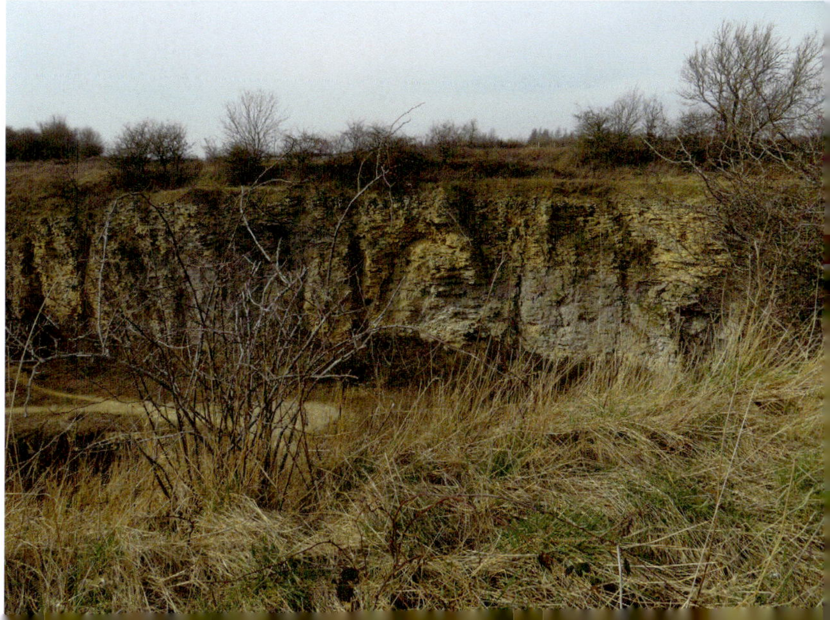

A quarry near Middridge off the path towards the railway and Middridge Grange.

around the quarry then looked over the edge but it was deep and silent, with heaps of stones and caves. There was nothing but the sound of rabbits scuttling over pebbles. He went on and completed eight circuits. Towards the end of the ninth he stood in his stirrups and shouted: 'Ye fairies, ye fairies, wi' your iron gads, Ye daren't come out and fight us Middridge lads!' 'Gads' in this context will be an antique term for 'spears'. According to Hartland:

> Scarcely had the last words escaped his lips ere he was nearly surrounded by many hundreds of the little folks, who are ever ready to revenge, with the infliction of the most dreadful Punishment, every attempt at insult. The most robust of the fairies, who I take to have been Oberon, their king, wielding an enormous javelin, thus, also in rhymes equally rough, rude, and rustic, addressed the witless wight:–
>
> 'Sillie Willy, mount thy filly;
> And if it isn't weel corn'd and fed,
> I'll hae thee afore thou gets hame to thy Midridge bed.'

It was fortunate for Willy that there was still light remaining. He struck his spurs into the sides of his beast and as he rode he threw bark behind him so that the fairy was forced to slow down and detour to avoid its magical powers. Finally, Willy could see a single poplar tree which marked the entrance to the farm. Now he only had a few tiny fragments of rowan left in the lining of his pocket, and desperately he turned these out to gain what seconds he could. As he came to a fence, he whipped his horse and she flew over like a bird. The stable door was wide open so he galloped in, to the amazement of the revellers. Once the door was closed, and as soon as Willy was able to draw his breath, he related to his friends a full account of his adventures.

The next morning it was discovered, to the amazement of all, that the iron javelin of the fairy king was stuck fast in the great oak door. It took the strength of the strongest member of the fraternity, and the help of a blacksmith's hammer, to drive it out. As far as foolhardy Willy was concerned, no one could persuade him ever again, for love nor money, to visit the fairies and invite them to Middridge!

Middridge Grange Farm stands on a long ridge (the 'mid-ridge') looking down on the railway. It is seventeenth century at least, and one of the oldest occupied buildings in the county. According to the current owner, the quarry in question was filled in long ago. As far as the javelin mark was concerned it could still be seen in a door until it was replaced by his grandfather. It is often claimed that the actual route of the Stockton and Darlington Railway was altered by George Stephenson to avoid the potential wrath of hordes of disturbed fairy folk. In reality the route was diverted to make use of stationary steam engines on the Brusselton Incline rather than expensive horsepower, which needed a more gradual incline. No fairies have been seen recently but the clanking smoking

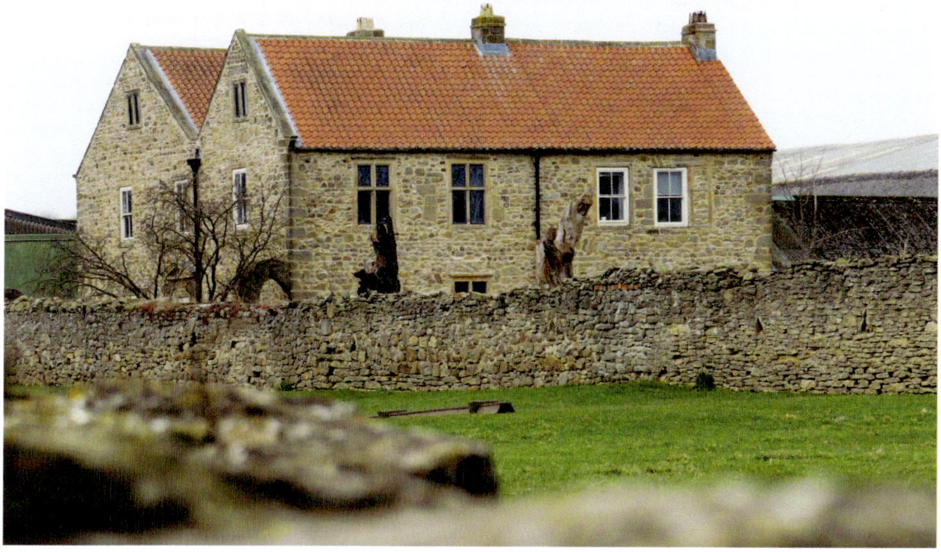

Middridge Grange farmhouse. One of the oldest buildings in County Durham which has been fully and tastefully restored by the current owners.

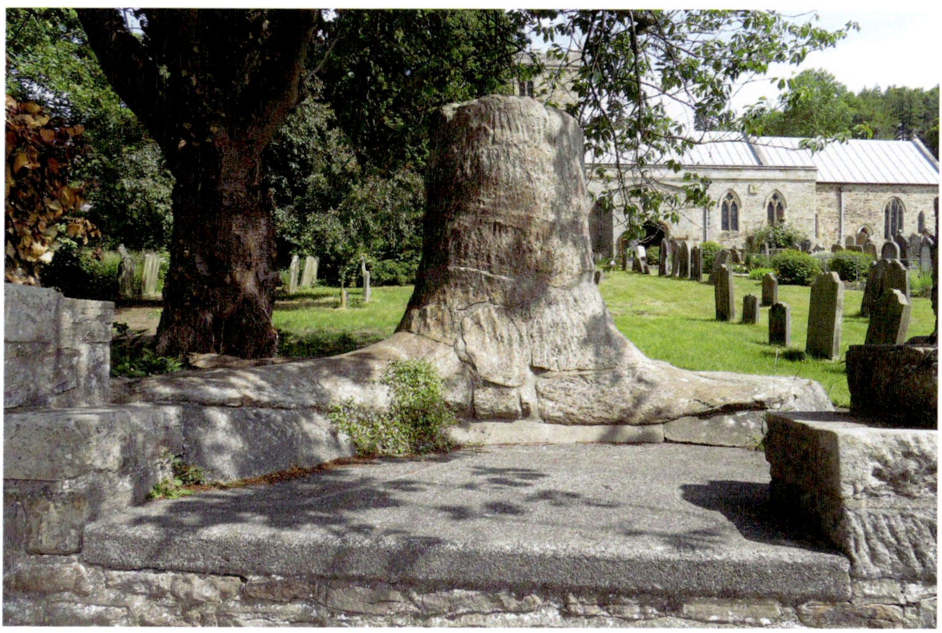

Unmistakeably Stanhope because of the famous fossilised tree trunk found by lead miners. Once it was a hotbed of sinister fairies, but now it is bustling hotspot for coffee-seeking tourists.

locomotives on the world-famous line probably forced them to relocate. Maybe to Stanhope?

One of the best fairy stories is set in lovely Weardale. In olden times, fairies could often be heard singing to the sound of the stream running over pebbles. They lived in caves deep in the hillside. Fairies are a jealous people who do not wish to be seen. In this case they were disturbed by a little girl gathering primroses. As she searched, she heard sounds of merriment coming from a little cave and ventured inside. To her amazement she saw the fairies and rushed home to tell her father. However, he knew the danger she was now in, and that the fairies would come for her to take her. So off he went to consult a local wise woman. She told him the fairies would come at midnight but would have no power if perfect silence was kept. Any noise would break that protection.

That night he locked the doors of stables and byres and cooped up the hens and turkeys. He fed the dogs bones to make them full and sleepy. He stopped the clocks and put out the fires. Then he sat waiting. Sure enough, the fairies came through the garden gate and rode up on their fairy ponies. Finding everything still, they paused. But the farmer had forgotten the little spaniel which slept at the foot of his daughter's bed. Hearing the tiny horse hoofs beneath the window, it barked furiously. When the farmer ran upstairs he discovered his daughter had gone.

The farmer returned to the witch. What he must do, she said, was to go to the cave carrying a sprig of rowan as protection against magic. He must also take three other items. The first was something that would give light without burning. The second was a chicken with no bone in its body. The third was an animal that would give part of its body without shedding one drop of blood. 'If', she said, 'you take these three things with you, the King of the Fairies cannot keep your daughter.'

Then the farmer left with some hope. As he walked along the lane he muttered the riddles. Then he met a beggar who over-heard his words and said: 'Can you help me, sir? I am old and I am poor and I have nothing to eat.' The farmer gave him sixpence and, in response, the beggar said: 'Now I will help you. The answer to your first question is – a glowworm. It will light your house but never burn.' Then the beggar vanished. The farmer continued. And as he looked ahead he noticed a thrush fleeing from a swooping kestrel. He picked up a stone and hurled it at the kestrel, driving it away. Then the thrush turned back and perched on a bush and it spoke. 'The answer to your second question – is an egg. An egg is a chicken without, as yet, a bone in its body.' Then the thrush sang three notes and flew off. On the farmer walked, musing about the third question. He heard some pitiful crying from a hedge, and saw a young rabbit trapped in a wire snare. He released it but instead of running off it spoke to him: 'Thank you for helping me, sir. Now I will help you with your question. The answer is – a lizard. If you catch it by its tail it will run off and leave the tail in your hand without shedding a drop of blood.' Then the rabbit disappeared.

The farmer went home and found an egg. He gathered three glowworms from a hedgerow. He wandered onto the moors and found a lizard basking on stones and he seized its tail. It ran off and left it in his hand. Then the farmer put a sprig of rowan in his hat and took the tokens to the cave. The fairies could not harm him of course because of the rowan. Then when he presented his three gifts, they were forced to give back his daughter. Never again did she spy on the fairies in their cave.

On the eastern edge of Stanhope is the pretty Shittlehope Burn. On the west side of the burn near the second bridge there are the so-called Fairy Holes. I'd say these are my first choice, although if you head towards Eastgate there is the much more impressive Fairy Holes Cave on the flank of Snowhope Moor.

We journey on over heather clad moors to the River Tees on the southern edge of County Durham to see a water sprite. The upper reaches are one of the most beautiful sights in the North Pennines. It is very dangerous in certain stretches but that is because of the nature of the river rather than the water sprites. It is claimed that in the depths of turmoil dwells a hag or sprite known as Peg Powler waiting to lure inquisitive children and adults into the murky waters. William Henderson describes Peg Powler as having green hair and 'an insatiable desire for human life'. With her long, water-drenched hair and frightening face she is said to be about when green foam – Peg Powler's suds – appears on the river's surface, or the finer foam known as Peg Powler's cream. Indeed, if you stare long enough into the turmoil I'll guarantee you will see her face fleetingly.

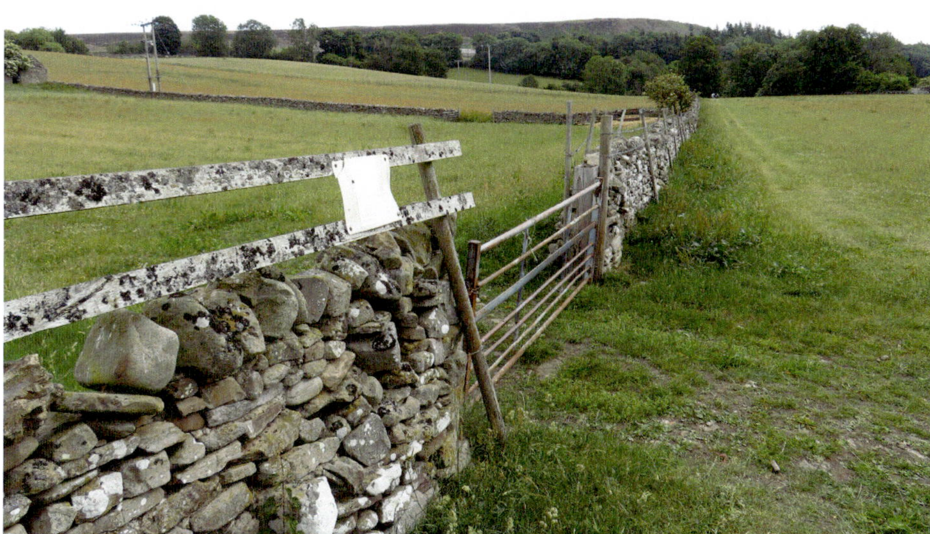

The route to the Fairy Holes beside the unfortunately named but attractive Shittlehope Burn.

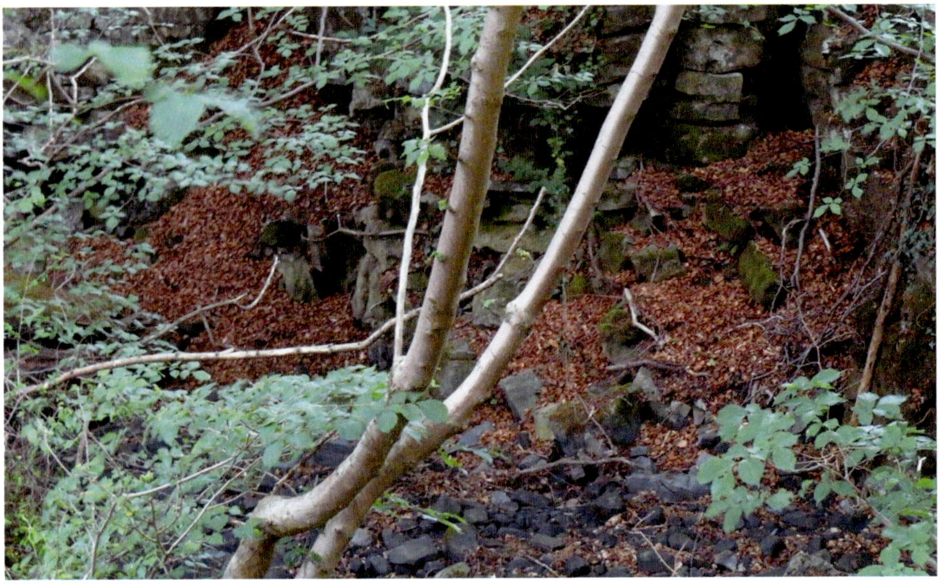

The Fairy Holes are, in truth, not much more than overhangs, but beggars can't be choosers when it comes to telling fairy tales.

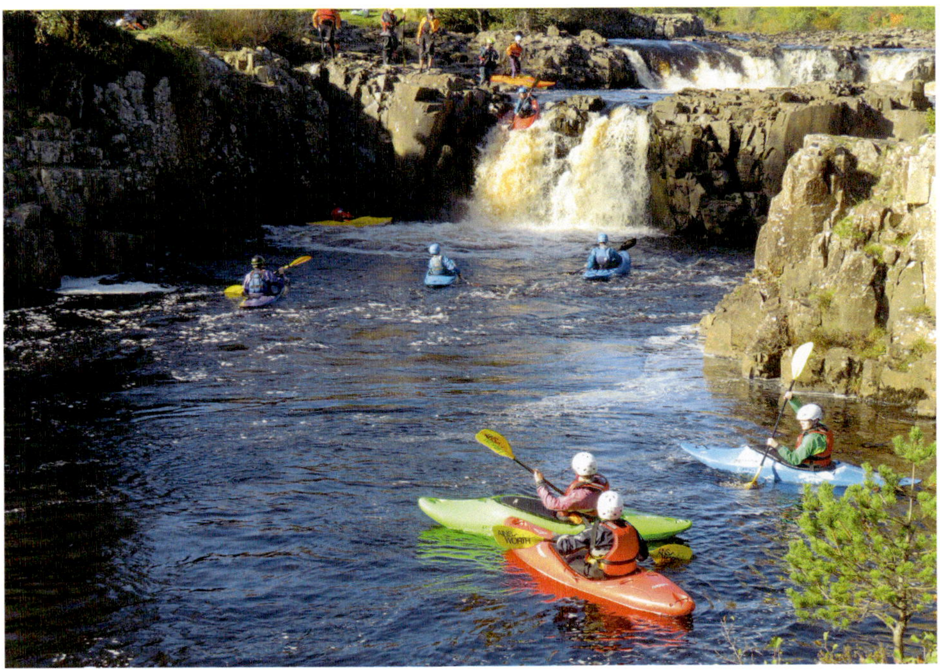

Low Force is somewhat eclipsed by its 70-foot-high senior partner High Force. They were formed where the Tees crosses the Whin Sill. I've seen Peg Powler here many times. Just be patient and stare into the foaming waters for a long time. These foolish canoeists at Low Force on the Tees are clearly oblivious to the threat posed by Peg.

Water sprite stories are very common and relate to river goddess worship, and the ritual sacrifice of young children to river gods and goddesses. The word 'sprite', incidentally, is derived from the Latin *spiritus* (spirit). Sunday is Peg Powler's favoured day for catching her prey. So perhaps the moral of the story, like the Lambton Worm, is that you should be at church on Sundays instead of idling away your time on a warm summer day enjoying the spectacular scenery of Upper Teesdale, the excellent coffee shop in the Bowlees Centre and the gift shops of Middleton!

Far away on the northern County Durham boundary the renowned Hedley Kow haunted the area around Hedley and Ebchester. It was a bogie, a sort of shape-shifting elf or brownie, perhaps related to the Cauld Lad of Hylton.

The mischievous creature played practical tricks on humans. Once it appeared before an old lady in the form of a truss of straw which she picked up and carried away. It became so heavy she had to put it down to catch her breath. The bale rose upright and vanished with a laugh and shout. On another occasion the bogie shift-shaped into a cow, led the milkmaid a merry dance round the field, during milking time upset the pail, slipped its tie and then vanished with a loud laugh. The Kow constantly imitated the voices of a servant-girl's lovers, overturned the kale-pot, gave the cream to the cats, unravelled knitting, or stopped the spinning-wheel working.

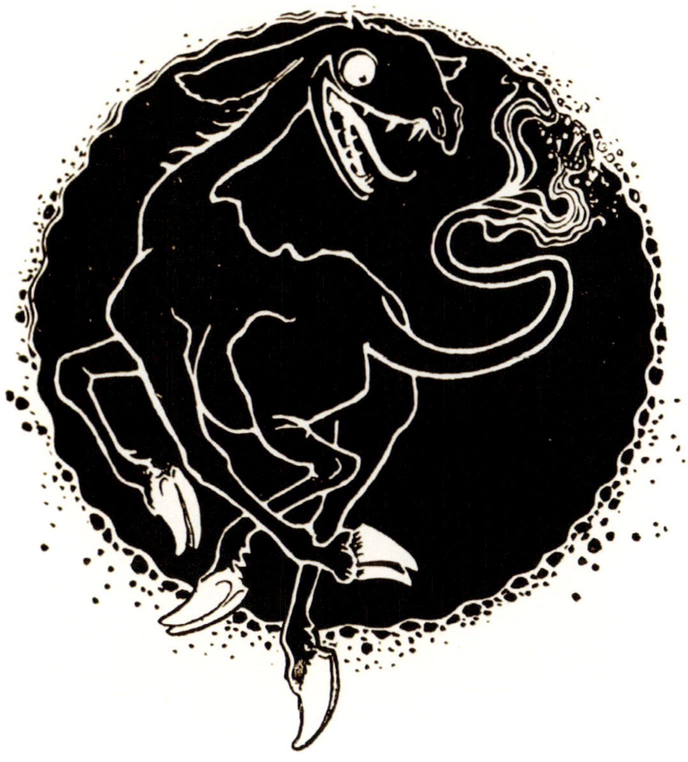

The Hedley Kow. (From *English Fairy Tales* by Joseph Jacobs, 1894. Illustration by John D. Batten).

But the creature did far worse things. He would mock the goodwife, and when her husband rushed with a stick to drive him away it would be snatched by an unseen hand and the husband would be beaten instead. Again, two young men of Newlands, near Ebchester, went to meet their sweethearts. Arriving at the trysting place, they saw them walking ahead. The lads followed, unable to overtake them, then found themselves up to the knees in a bog to the loud amusement of their true beguiler. The men got clear and ran homewards, the Kow at their heels hooting and mocking. Crossing the Derwent they fell into the water, mistook each other for the sprite, and finally reached home to tell their fearful tale.

Then there is the Picktree (or Pelton, or Portobello) Brag. In old sources, brags, or goblins, are often described as Boggles, hence the term 'Bogie Man'. This one often appeared as an ass. Whoever mounted it was carried off then thrown into a bog or gorse bush. The creature would then run off laughing mischievously. Sir Cuthbert Sharp interviewed a knowledgeable old Pelton woman about it. She said that it often appeared in the form of a calf which, for some reason, had a white handkerchief around its neck. It had a bushy tail and galloped like a 'Gallowa' or pit pony. It was attracted by her husband's white suit but when he attempted to mount it, the beast threw him into a pond. I can think of good practical reasons though as to why a husband might invent a tale to justify his bemired best suit. The A1(M) motorway was built in the vicinity of Picktree and may have scared it off for good.

7

A Coven of Witches

The gentry of Easington hunted hares regularly. However, the coursing did not go well because every time a certain hare, darker and greyer in colour, was started the crafty creature twisted and turned so artfully that the bemused, blundering dogs were invariably thrown off the scent and the hare got clear away. The men spent many muddy hours tramping through woods and undergrowth searching for their lost harriers. Eventually it seemed that they would have to give up their sport.

One of the hunters eventually came up with the theory that the hare must be a witch in disguise. Force was added to this view by knowledge that a certain local hovel occupied by an ill-natured old hag was always locked up when the sports were held. It never occurred to the huntin', shootin' and fishin' fraternity that this was because the old lady had to work in the fields to scrape a living. None of her neighbours would work alongside her. They claimed she was a witch, and since the hare was undoubtedly a witch, the identity was obvious.

The hare-hunters acquired a bloodhound sensitive to the smell of women (you have to wonder about the motivation of the trainer...). This led the next hunt, and when the hare was sighted it was closely followed. As always, it headed towards Easington but this time it could not throw the hounds off the scent. It ran over the village green to a little stone cottage. Then it shot towards a hole at the bottom of the door. Just before it got through, the hound was able to seize and tear away a piece of flesh from its haunch. The huntsmen broke down the door and were aghast at the sight. There sat the witch, sweating and shivering after the chase and bleeding from her leg which she was hastily bandaging. The drawing of blood had broken her charm, and her power was forever gone.

In fact, this story ends happily – well sort of! The huntsmen were so taken by her appeals that they took pity and left her alone. From then on, the merry gentlemen went on tearing innocent wildlife to fragments.

Apparently, the old woman continued to live in the village. According to Brockie (who was told the story by a Mrs Mary Shaw) she was 'endowed with all those unamiable qualities of the virago that are best calculated to keep a countryside in fear'. When she died, she was buried in the churchyard despite having never attended church. However, in the form of a white sheep rolling over and over on the churchyard wall, she continued to terrorise the villagers. The reliable Mrs Shaw actually witnessed this herself – and no doubt enjoyed many a glass of port as she regaled her cronies with this astonishing tale. It's a good story – too good to be wasted. In fact, a near identical story is linked to Sedgefield.

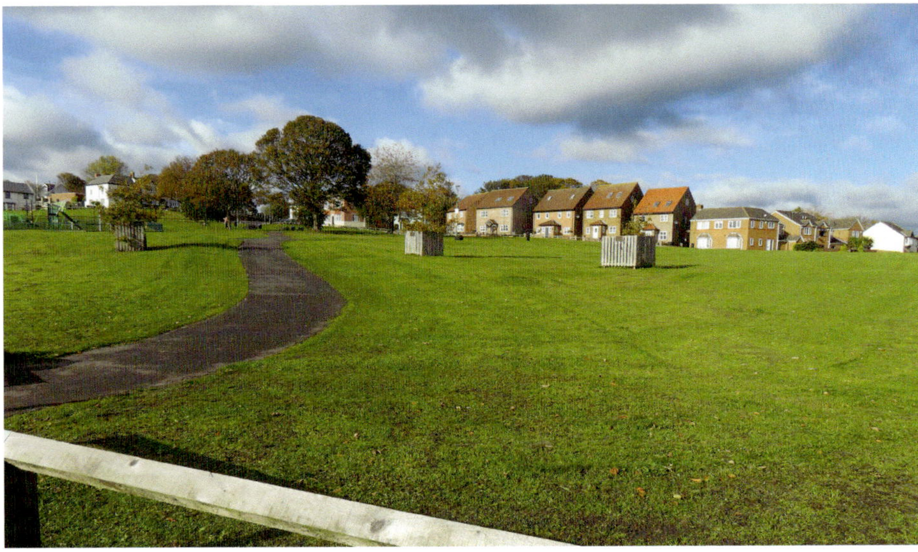

The extensive Easington village green across which the shape-shifted witch sprinted towards her humble cottage. She would be amazed to learn that she was to become, for a time, the site of a café called the Easington Hare.

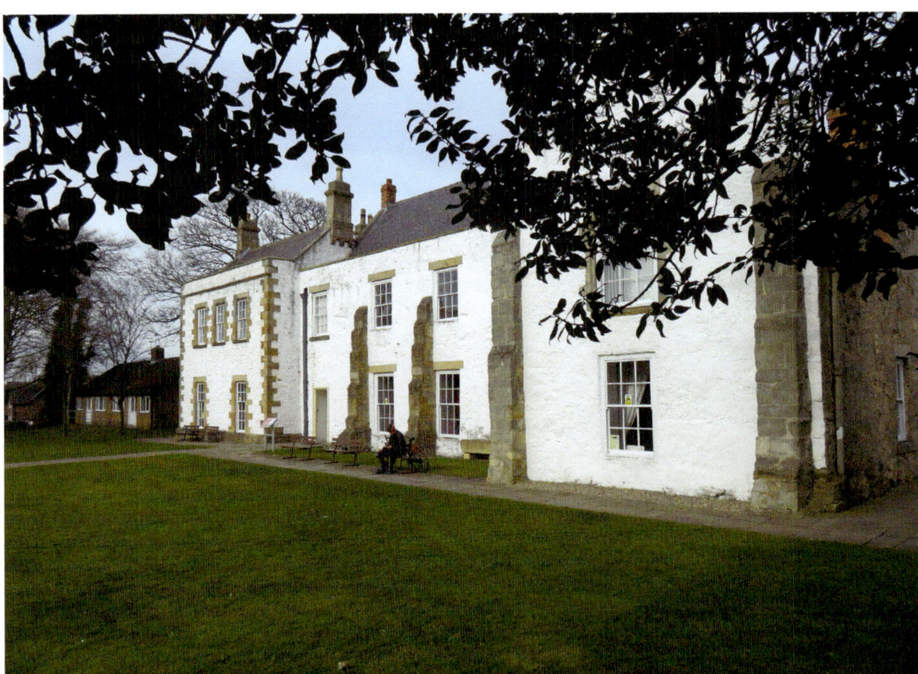

Seaton Holme Hall dates back to the early medieval period and must have witnessed the hunting of the shape-shifted witch/hare. It's one of the oldest secular domestic buildings in the county.

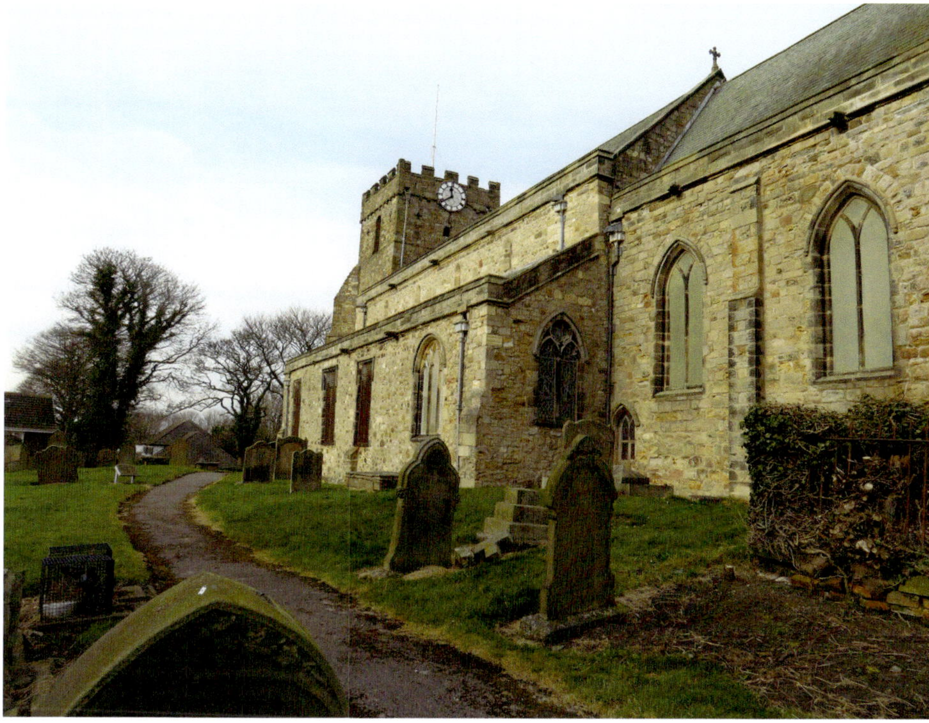

St Mary the Virgin in Easington is a fine Norman church overlooking the village and surrounded by a 6-foot-high wall. It was along that very wall that the Easington witch/hare was seen rolling in the form of a sheep.

Hares figure in folk tales in many countries. Boudicca carried a pet hare and when she let it run free, its path was read as an omen. Shape-shifting witch/hares are very common. For centuries, people believed that witches could change into animals such as hares, ravens and cats and back again. The famous Scottish witch Isobel Gowdie from Auldearn, burnt alive in 1662, recounted an incident in which she was chased by hounds as a hare until eventually able to hide in a house. The hounds found her, and she recited the spell that changed her back into a human. It was held to be true well into the nineteenth century that witches, if injured when in their animal form, would display this injury when they changed back into their human selves.

Witch hunts emerge primarily in the period after the Protestant Reformation. The most prominent example of the mass hysteria of witch persecution in County Durham was in Washington in the late seventeenth century when poor old Jane Atkinson met her fate.

In 1696 Washington was a small, inward-looking farming settlement around the old hall. A devastating disease resulted in the death of all of the cattle which inspired a wave of hysteria and the pursuit of scapegoats at a time when people regarded misfortune as the result of God's will or dark forces. An elderly woman called Jane Atkinson who lived alone was seized, accused and 'tested'. This involved sealing her in a sack and throwing her into water to see if she would float. If she floated, she was guilty since her evil meant she was rejected by God and could not be baptised. If she sank it meant she was innocent. You see the problem immediately of course?

So, Jane was tied into a sack and thrown into the Washington Pond (now the village war memorial) and, disappointingly, sank. So – the best out of three! Inevitably poor Jane was drowned. It is claimed that the burial register did have the word 'witch' written next to her name, but it does not survive. She is said to be buried in Washington Churchyard, and local people have convinced themselves that an illegible eighteenth-century gravestone marks the spot. Her bedraggled and distraught ghost can still be seen though, usually after closing time at the two nearby public houses.

The Derwent Valley, though, was awash with witches busily communing with familiars and shapeshifting. On 9 April 1673, Ann Armstrong gave testimony at Morpeth that she had attended meetings of witches at various locations. She named those in attendance and described them dancing: 'In the likenesse of haires, some in the likenesse of cats and others in the likenesse of bees.' She had met the Devil at these dances, and the Devil made the group confess the evil deeds they had done. Confessions included the killing of neighbours' animals and children by bewitching them.

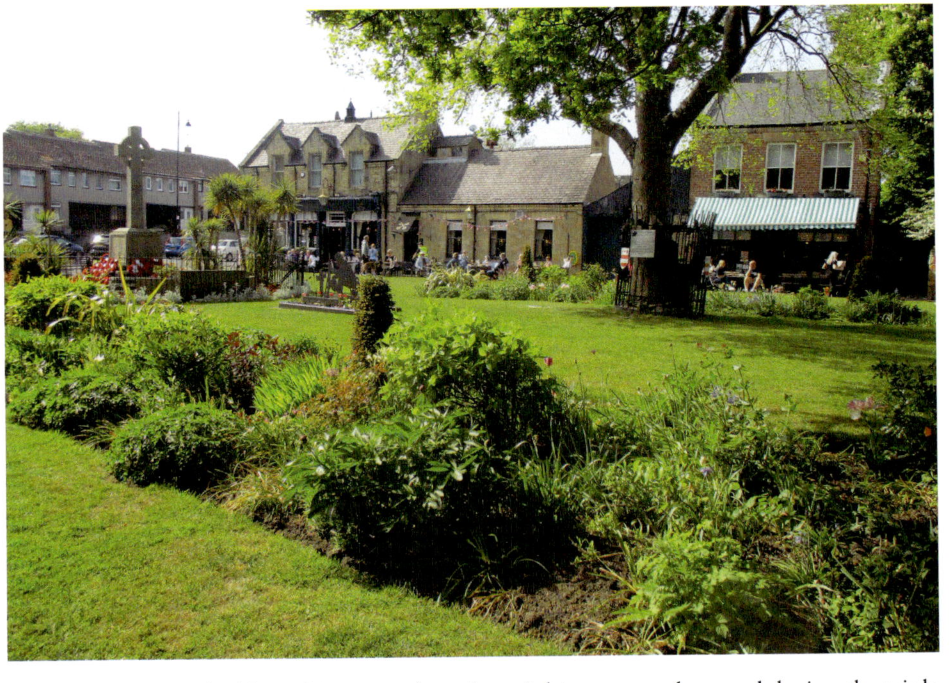

The village green of Old Washington, where Jane Atkinson was drowned during the triple testing of her as a suspected witch.

One odd piece of 'evidence' is the gravestone of Elizabeth Lee, said to be the last of a long line of witches who was buried in the grounds of St Edmund's Church in 1792. Not much is known about Lee, who was from 'the Riding', an area of moorland now submerged beneath the water of Derwent Reservoir. She was married to John, who died in 1771, and she was rumoured to practice witchcraft. However, she was never proven guilty and she died at the very old age of eighty-seven. Terrified locals were so afraid that she wouldn't rest peacefully that the vicar installed an Eye of God stained-glass window to ward off forces of evil. The fearful parishioners surrounded St Edmund's with wild garlic, which provides protection against witches, so her spirit could never be conjured from the final resting place of her body. The controversy surrounding Lee's burial within the holy grounds of the church continued long after her death, and her headstone was eventually brought inside. The stone now hangs beneath the Eye of God on the west wall of St Edmund's. The Eye of God is unusual and indicates that the vicar was a freemason. Elizabeth's body still lies in the ground somewhere in the churchyard. There have been no recent sightings, so the garlic may be working.

Crooked Oak farmhouse near the oddly named Wallish Walls and overlooking the River Derwent. This was the home of the notorious witch Jane Frizzle. There is even a claim that she was hanged inside her own cottage but that seems to be based entirely upon the existence of a hook above the fireplace, which was used for quite innocent purposes. She is said to be buried near a crossroads on the busy A68 at Greenhead Farm, not far off.

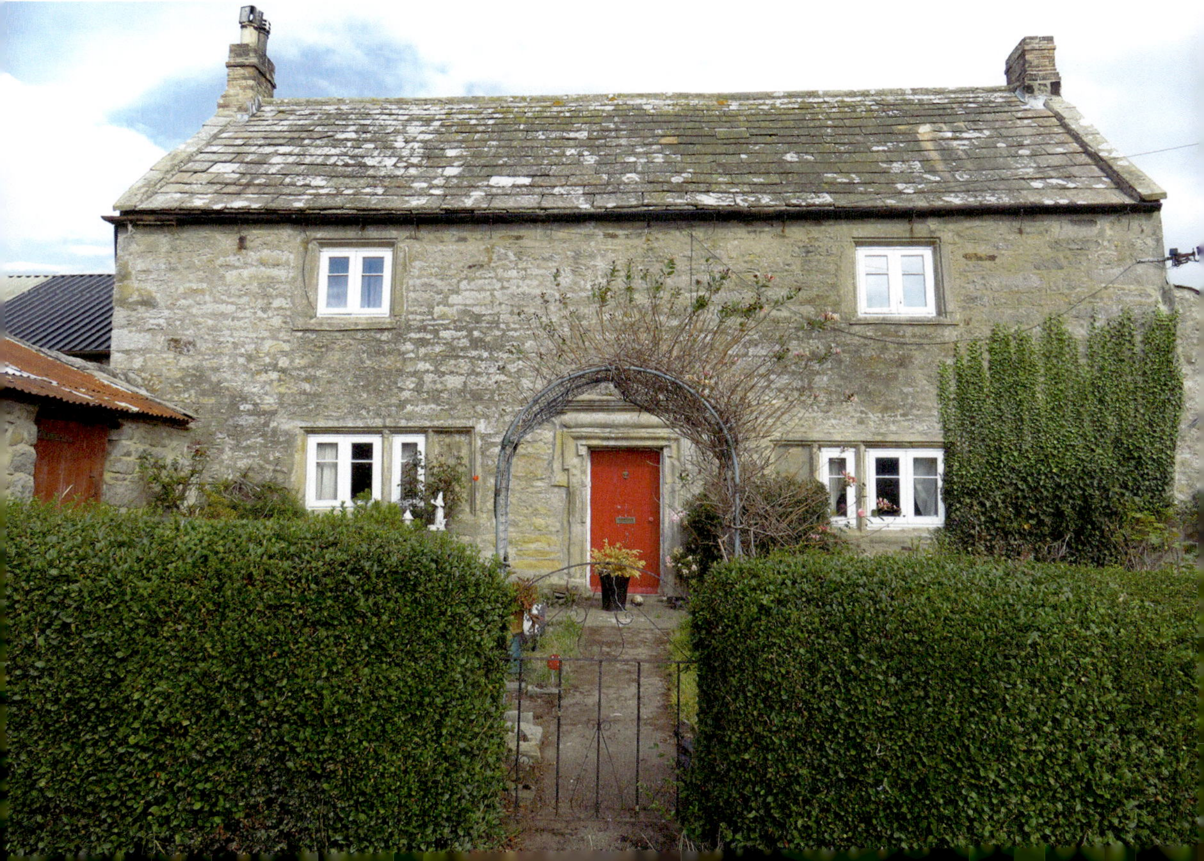

Not far off is a seventeenth-century farmhouse by the name of Crooked Oak, in one of the most beautiful spots in the Derwent Valley near the hamlet of Wallish Walls. It was said to be a hotbed of witchcraft in the sixteenth and seventeenth centuries. It has the date 1684 above the ornamented door. Jane Frizzle, one of Crooked Oak's inhabitants, was known as a witch. It was said she flew upon her broomstick at night, casting spells on men, maidens, and cattle. Frizzle was eventually tried and executed and is said to be buried in a field at Greenhead Farm in the Carterway Heads section near a significant crossroads of the modern A68 and the road linking Blanchland to Edmundbyers and Consett. That's where I would bury a witch anyhow! With a stake driven through her body to stop her rising.

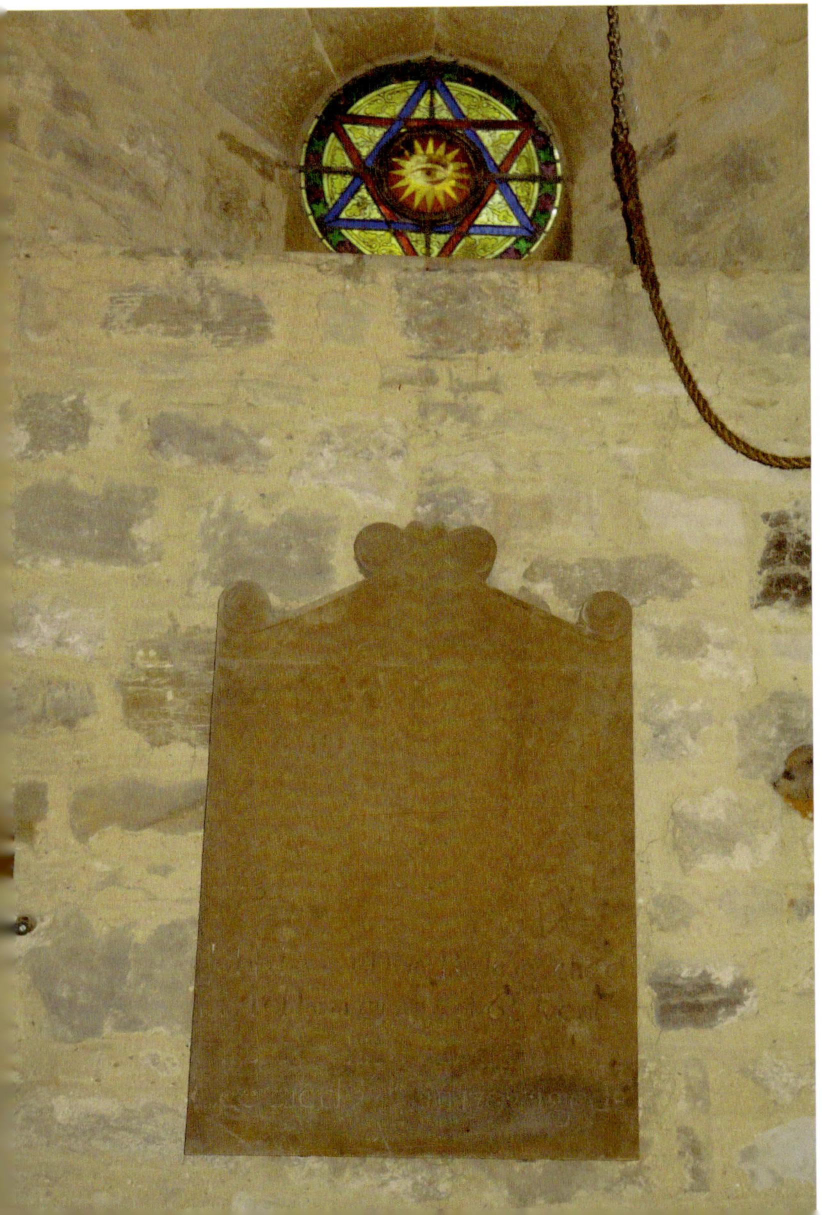

The Lee gravestone on the wall of St Edmund's Church is below the curious God's Eye circular window. Elizabeth was buried in the churchyard, and her name is at the bottom of the gravestone.

8

Holier than Thou!

County Durham is also notable for having strong links with three great Christian saints. Foremost is the Monty Pythonesque legend of the founding of the city and its great cathedral.

The twelfth-century chronicler Symeon of Durham recounts that in 875 the Danes took the monastery of Lindisfarne and the monks fled, carrying St Cuthbert's body with them. After seven years' wandering, it found a resting place at Chester-le-Street until 995. Another Danish invasion led to the removal of the body to Ripon. However, during an attempt to return it to Chester-le-Street the bier became trapped in mud at Warden Law. Despite all attempts, it could not be budged. Aldhun, Bishop of Chester-le-Street decreed a holy fast of three days, accompanied by prayers to the saint. Then Saint Cuthbert appeared to the monk Eadmer with instructions that the coffin should be taken to Dun Holm.

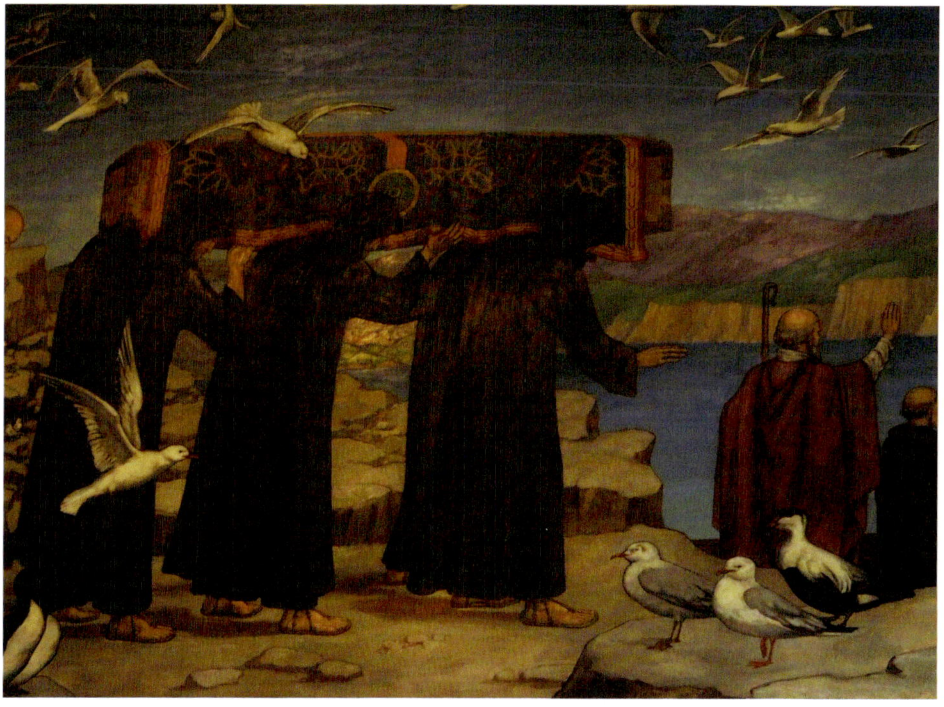

Paintings in St Mary and St Cuthbert's Church in Chester-le-Street tell the story of the travels of St Cuthbert and the founding of the city Durham and the cathedral. In this one the body of St Cuthbert starts its prolonged journey when the Danish raids begin. The artist is unknown.

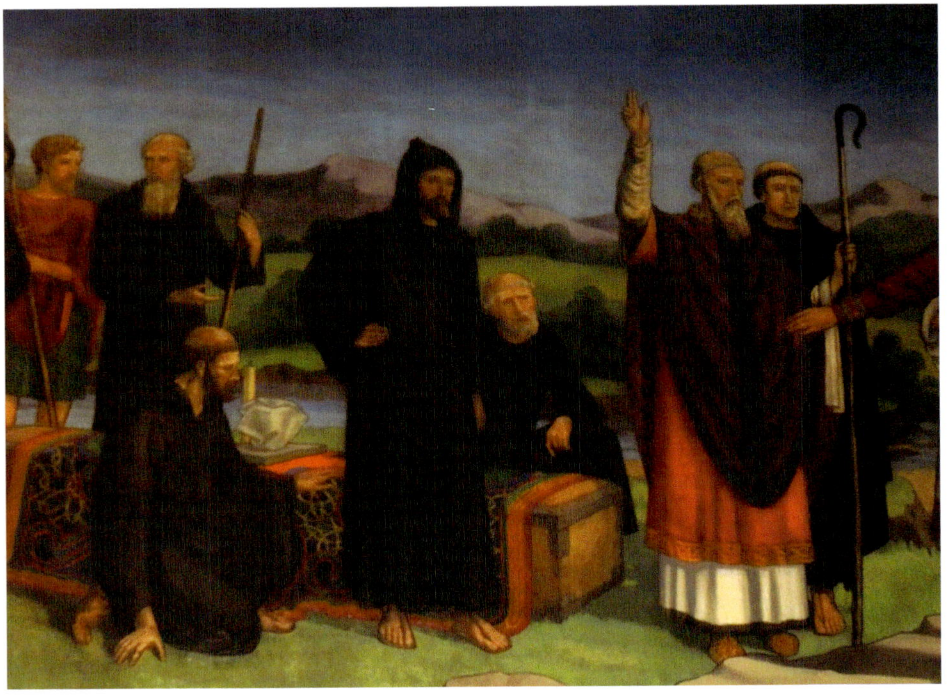

Another of the series of images in St Mary and St Cuthbert's in Chester-le-Street. The entourage have paused with the coffin of St Cuthbert and are, no doubt, waiting for spiritual guidance from any random passing milkmaid.

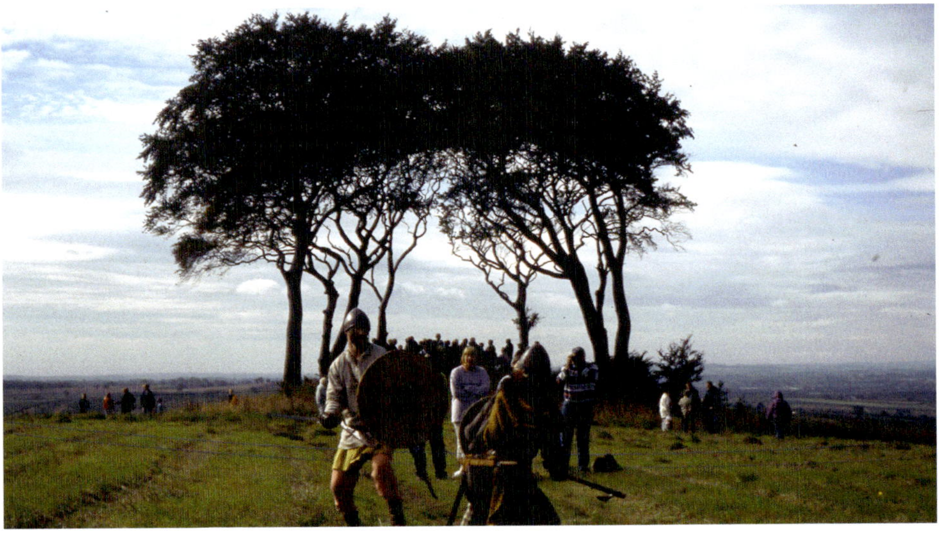

The Seven Sisters of Copt Hill at Houghton is a circle of six beech trees (five and a half really) on a burial mound where, allegedly, St Cuthbert's entourage rested. It is actually a very old Neolithic/Mesolithic burial mound. It is conveniently near the Copt Hill Inn with its varied menu, so I can see why they might hesitate here.

The entourage then discovered that the cart was miraculously free, but the next ordeal was that they did not know where Dun Holm was. By chance they came across a wandering milkmaid at Mount Joy seeking her lost dun cow last seen, she said, at Dun Holm. The monks, realising that this was a sign, followed her. They settled at a 'wooded hill-island formed by a tight gorge-like meander of the River Wear'. When they arrived at the destination, they erected a 'White Church'. Nothing of it survives today, having been supplanted by the marvelous Norman cathedral. Symeon claims this was the first building in the city, but may have meant in a supercilious way, the first stone building.

The curious story about town planning on the basis of corpse-bearing itinerants stalking a young woman seems to have been a total fabrication and a late addition. In fact, there were excellent political reasons for the St Cuthbert's Community to have chosen Durham. Bishop Aldhun's daughter was married to Uchtred, the Earl of Northumbria. From Uchtred's point of view, the relic would provide the reason, and perhaps the finances, for the construction of defensive works on the neck of the peninsula. Having St Cuthbert in his possession would bring him tremendous prestige, and pilgrims would bring money. The next of my chosen sites and saints is only a few miles away from the great city.

The monastic complex of Finchale Abbey is set in idyllic surroundings (apart from its proximity to Frankland Prison!). It is renowned for the mystical hermit

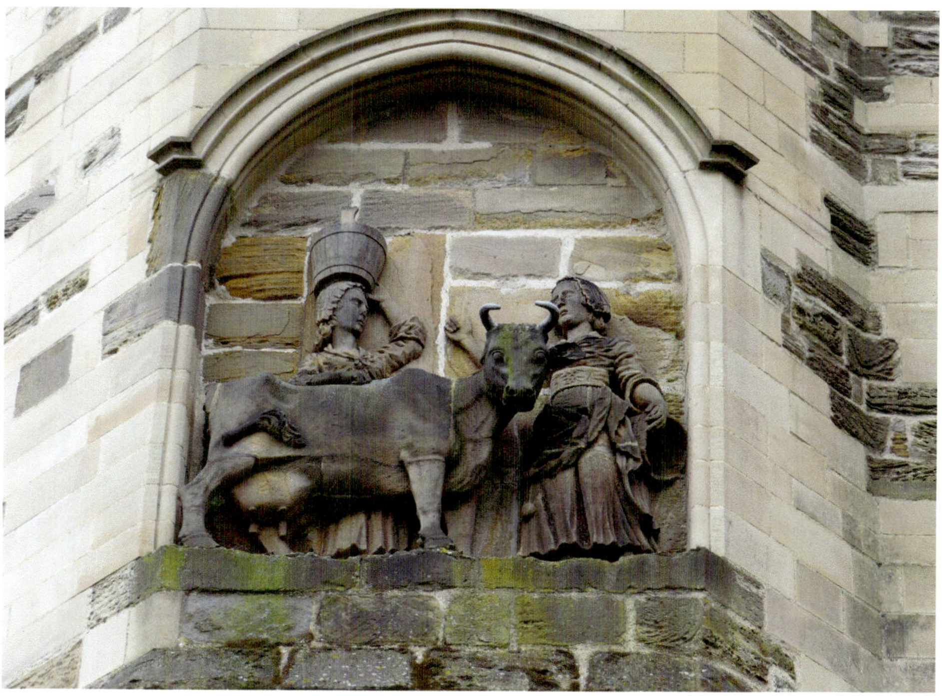

An eighteenth-century panel on the north façade of the cathedral depicts the legend of the Dun Cow and the cow-seeking milkmaid.

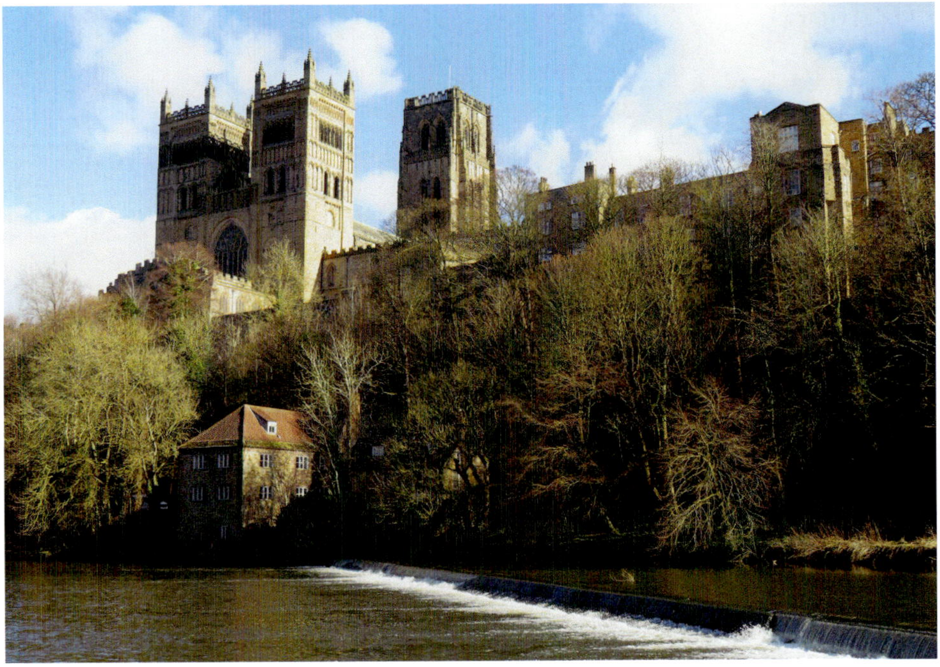

The classic view of Durham Cathedral from the south bank of the River Wear. The building directly opposite is a former fulling mill. Durham Cathedral is one of the finest examples of Romanesque architecture and is a UNESCO World Heritage Site. St Cuthbert and the Venerable Bede are buried there and have become major tourist attractions. They must be turning in their graves at the thought.

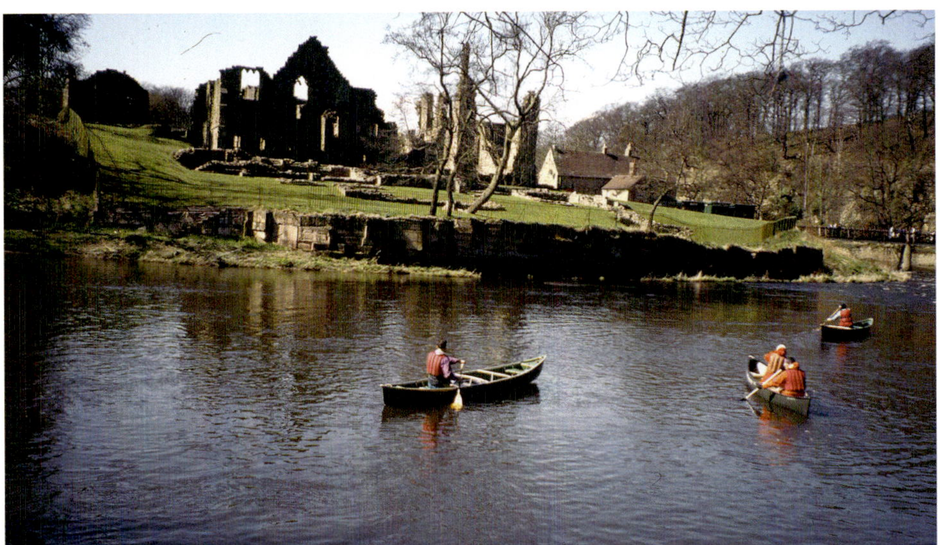

The scenic Finchale Abbey seen from the far side of the River Wear. It was founded in 1196 by the Benedictines of Durham City.

and saint who once lived there. Godric was born in Norfolk to poor parents somewhere between 1065 and 1072. He worked as a pedlar before going to sea. He became a ship's captain, a merchant and possibly a pirate for a time. He sold his boat and became a pilgrim. He did penances at shrines across England and travelled to Rome and the Holy Land. He eventually headed north living as a mendicant before finally arriving in Durham.

In a story suspiciously like the Dun Cow, the search for his spiritual home ended after a chance meeting with two shepherds talking of taking their flocks to Finchale which is where he believed St Cuthbert was directing him. On arrival he disappeared into the dense woodland where he was to spend the next sixty years. This Robinson Crusoe of faith levelled a plot of land, built himself a cabin and survived on herbal roots and foliage before raising crops. Throughout his life he ignored the plentiful game and fish in the area in favour of a frugal life. His struggle against fleshly temptations led to his standing naked in river water as he recited prayers and psalms, a fanatical dietary habit and cold-shouldering unannounced visitors. At one point he was visited by marauding Scottish soldiers around 1138, during the so-called Anarchy. They beat him and threatened to behead him, before destroying his hut and chapel and making their way back north.

He became renowned for his famous cures which embraced a wide range of ailments including fevers, tumours, heavy bleeding, hearing loss, miscarriages and post-natal problems. His 'medicines' included tiny pieces of bread or fragments of cloth torn from his perished belt – all personally blessed. Amongst some very famous Godric miracles was his Lazarus-like bringing to life of a dead child brought to him by a frantic couple after three days of prayer. He made the parents swear many times that while he lived they would never divulge any part of the incident. They kept their promise, and Godric only divulged his secret to his biographer near the end of his life. In the years after his death, Godric was responsible for no fewer than a further 225 miracles.

Ironically, while he deliberately sought out an isolated and austere existence he became a target for senior clergymen and religious scholars from across England. During his last years he became, allegedly, a confidant of the Archbishop of Canterbury. Although he and Beckett never physically met, they communicated, apparently, in secret, their messages relayed verbally by clergymen. Godric predicted the Archbishop would be forced to flee into exile after a row with the king, and some years later he again accurately forecast Beckett would be pardoned by the monarch. Godric also made many predictions of impending floods, disorder, famine, happiness and deaths.

When Brother Reginald sought Godric's endorsement of a book about his life, Godric reluctantly gave it after Reginald promised 'never to speak of these things here written nor show them to anyone' until the day following the hermit's burial. Godric finally died, after an extraordinarily action-packed life, on 21 May 1170. The lovely Finchale Priory was founded on the site of the hermit's grave and thrived for 350 years until Henry VIII dissolved the monasteries. The romantic ruins are now in the care of English Heritage.

One final point. St Godric, like St Cuthbert, hated and feared women. Yet strangely enough one of the stone benches in the chapter house is said to help women to become pregnant if they sit upon it. However, I'm not sure which one it is, so you might try them all.

As if St Cuthbert and St Godric are not enough, there is, of course, the Venerable Bede. Bede entered the twin monastery of St Peter's at Monkwearmouth and St Paul's at Jarrow at the age of seven and became one of the most learned men in Europe. He wrote many books, especially the *Ecclesiastical History of the English People*, and to the very last moment of his life was still busy translating part of the Bible into the Anglo-Saxon language. He is buried in Durham Cathedral. He was canonised in 1899, although he is still generally known as the Venerable Bede. The title 'Venerable' seems to have originated from the ninth century and means, in this case, 'revered' or 'esteemed'. However, an old story about the origin of the title is told by Grice.

Near the end of his life Bede was nearly blind. He continued his work, however, dictating to a team of scribes. He also, apparently, continued to preach to ordinary people, wandering along lanes and field edges to different venues. It was during one of these excursions that his title was born.

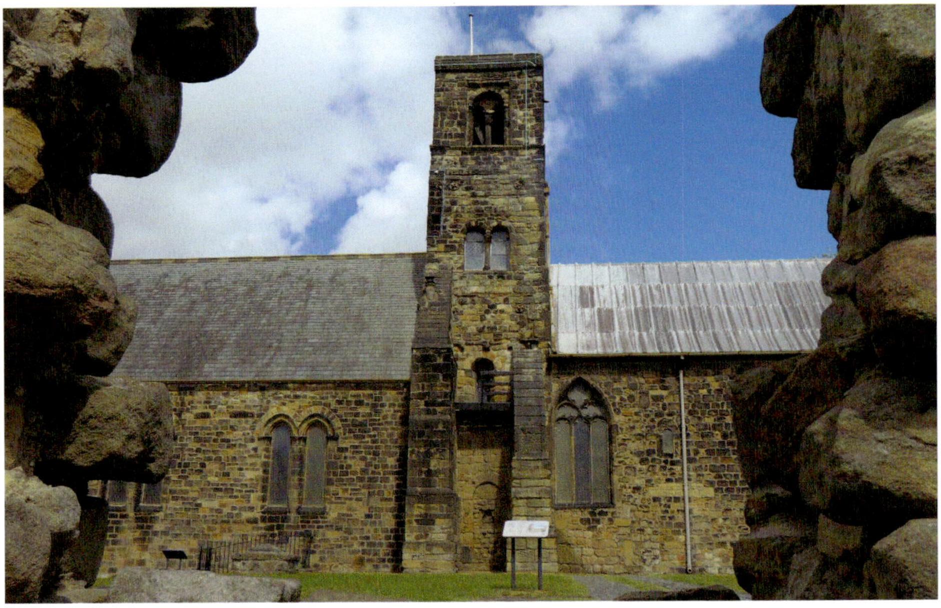

St Paul's at Jarrow was one of twin monastic campuses founded by Benedict Biscop. The Venerable Bede was originally buried at Jarrow. He was moved to Durham in 1022. His remains were allegedly stolen by a Durham monk, a collector of relics, and were removed to Durham Cathedral for safety. I'd have thought that South Tyneside Council had a good case for demanding restoration.

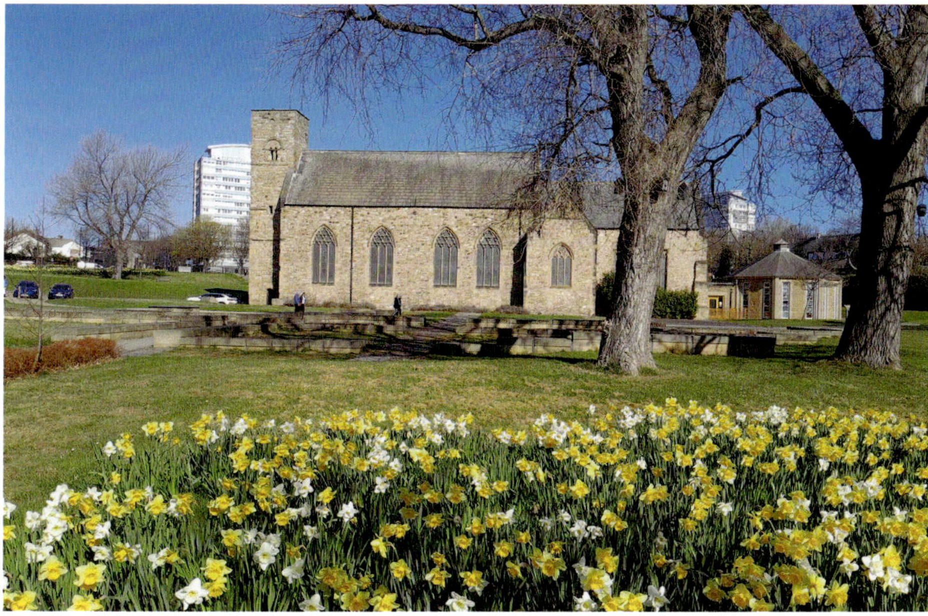

St Peter's Church in Monkwearmouth was a twin campus with St Paul's of Jarrow, founded by the Saxon nobleman and ex-warrior Benedict Biscop.

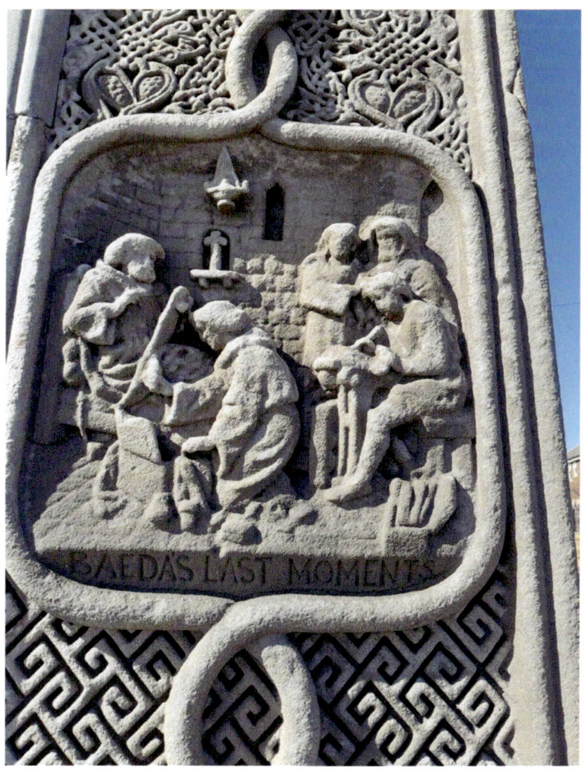

The north face features eleven religious figures. The south face is embellished with birds, animals and vine patterns. The east face is a series of panels about Bede's life. His last moments are shown here. He is still dictating to meet his publishers' deadline presumably.

It is said that as he walked he was seen by a local boy who had nothing better to do than play a prank. He approached Bede and said: 'Father, a crowd of people have sent me to you to ask you to go and to preach the gospels to them. I've been sent to guide you to them.' Bede replied: 'You are kind my son. I must ask you to lead me since I am blind and cannot find my way myself to your people.' The boy led him to a lonely corner where there was nothing but grass, hawthorn bushes and piles of stones. 'Here,' he said, 'here is your congregation. Waiting upon your words.' And he was barely able to restrain his sniggering.

So Bede prayed. Then he began his sermon. He preached about the Creation and the birth of Christ. He spoke about the meaning of the life of Jesus. Then he told of the Crucifixion and about the ascension of Jesus to Heaven. But only a chuckling boy could hear the marvellous words. As he sat, the boy was thinking that when the old man finished he would leap up and tell him that he had been talking to himself and would run off leaving him there. When Bede ended his sermon and sat to rest, the air was filled with a thousand voices crying 'Amen, Venerable Bede.' The boy leapt up and looked around. He could see no one else but him and the old man. The chant continued and now the boy realised that the sound was coming from the grass, and the trees and the stones. Even he was moved at the response to the sermon he had mocked. Ashamed of himself, he asked pardon from Bede then led him back to the monastery. From that day onward the boy always spoke of the Venerable Bede, and soon everyone around him began to use that title. Bede was finally canonised in 1899. Presumably he was in a queueing system.

In the next chapter we move seamlessly on from men of God to the Devil and all his works.

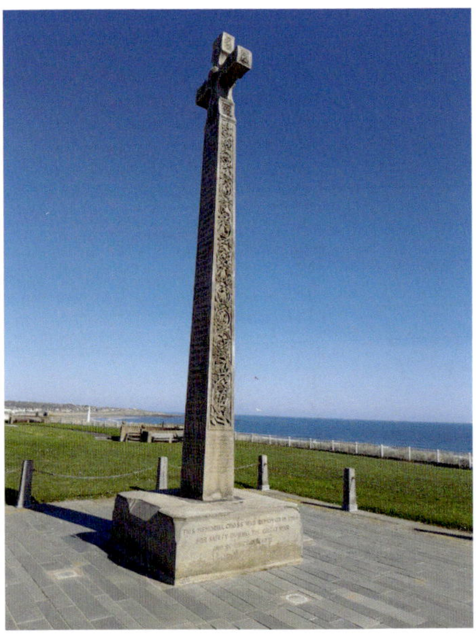

The Bede Memorial Cross created by Charles Clement Hodges was unveiled in 1904 in Cliff Park. It commemorates the life of the Venerable Bede.

9
Oddities and the Devil

My title is a thin disguise for 'bits and pieces' – stories that don't easily fit into the other themes but are, indisputably, odd.

One of the oddest County Durham tales is the story about the hanging of the monkey. It is simple enough. During wartime, a French ship was wrecked off Hartlepool Headland. This may have been in the 1790s when there was a particular concern with the threat of French invasion. Anyhow the story has no time frame. The fishermen of Hartlepool, like some sort of self-appointed army patrol, observed the death struggles of the vessel. Concerned that there might be survivors needing help, they went off to search the wreckage washed ashore. In fact, their motive could well have been very different. Looting wrecked vessels was a nice source of income in those times.

Hartlepool Headland. Perhaps the French vessel from which the monkey emerged was wrecked here. This is the real, original Hartlepool as opposed to modern West Hartlepool.

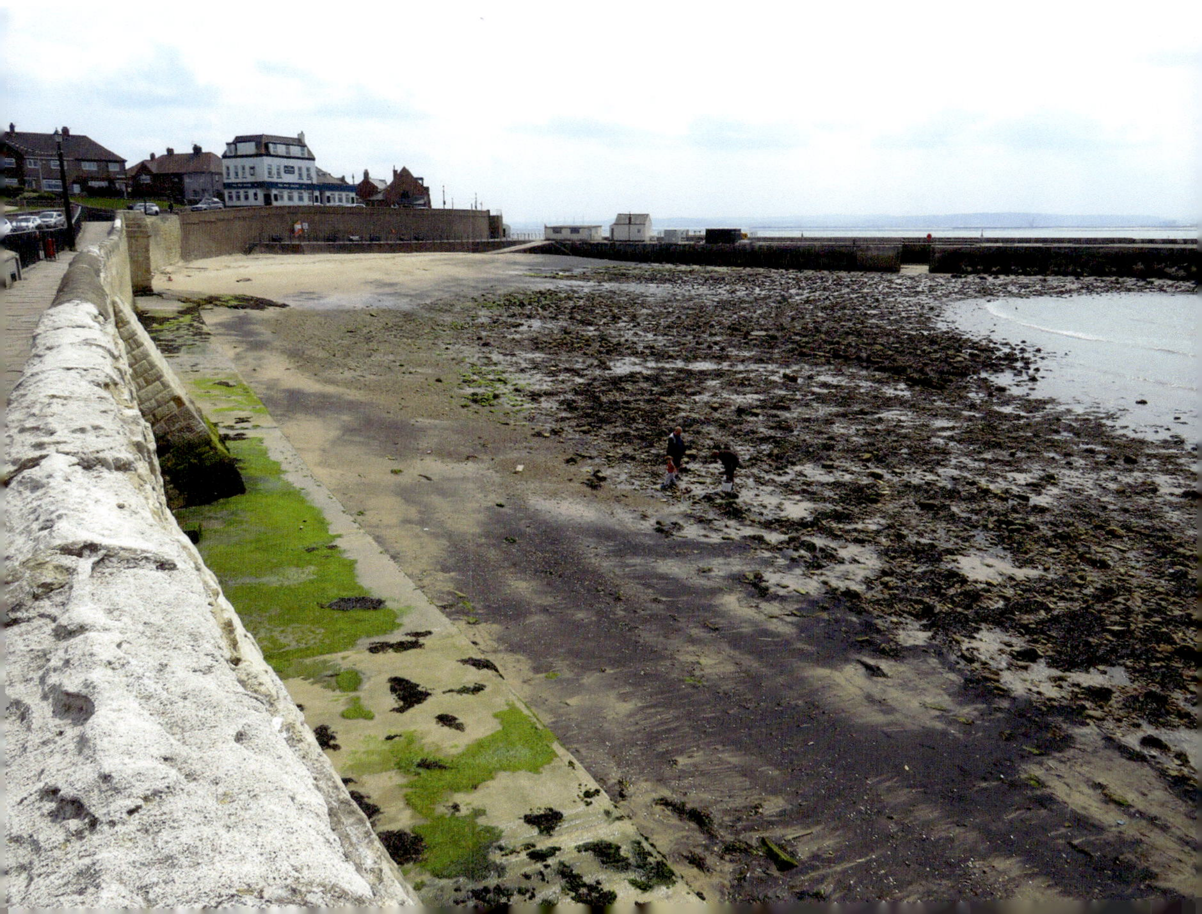

All they found was someone dressed in a sort of travesty of French sailor's dress. It had to be French of course because they had never actually met a French person. They seized the unfortunate creature and dragged it off for trial. It was, of course, a monkey, a pet of the French crew. After interrogating the monkey, which merely gabbled away in the incomprehensible nonsense which the French always speak, they decided that this was indeed a French spy. They found it guilty. They cobbled together a gallows on the beach and hanged the monkey forthwith.

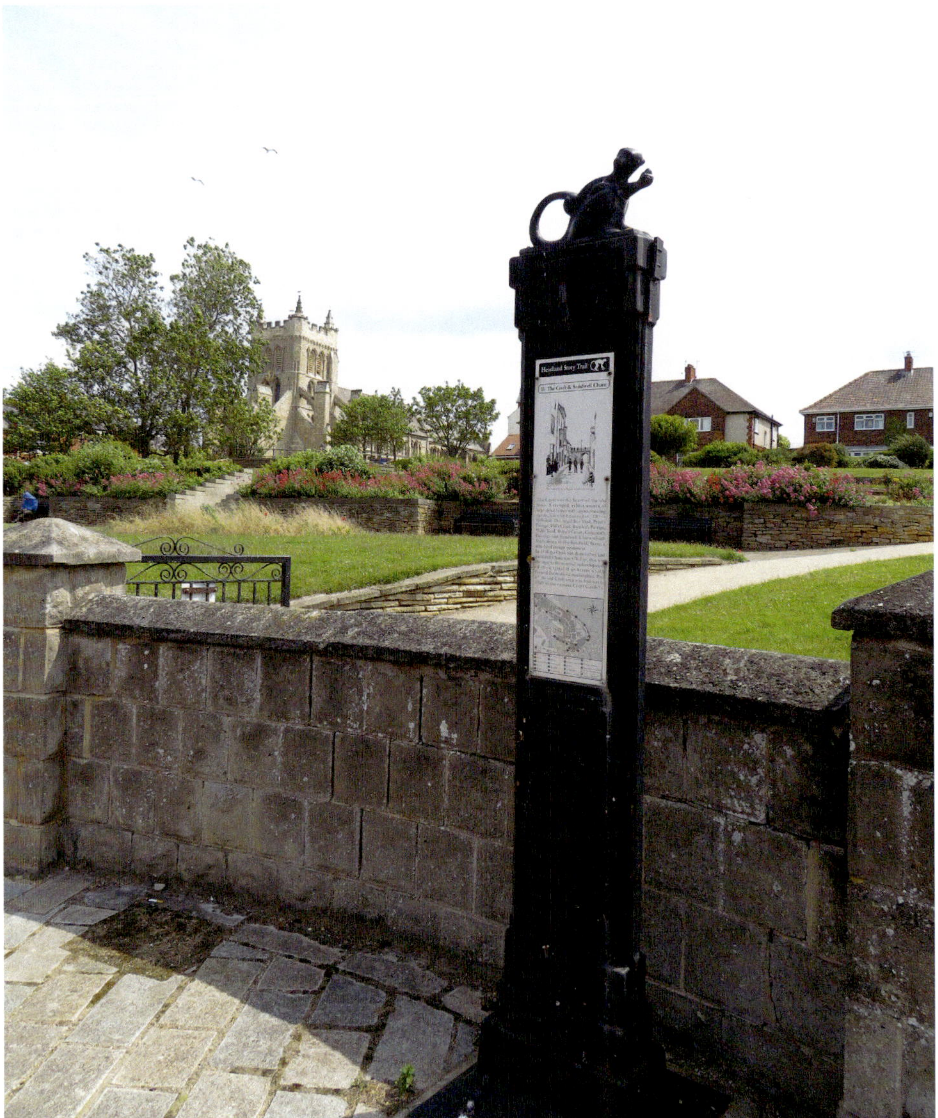

A version of the poor monkey is used to identify a series of excellent heritage boards on historic Hartlepool Headland.

People from towns in the North East have long mocked the honest folk of Hartlepool for their supposed ignorance. Over time 'Who hanged the monkey' has been used as a very loud football chant by opponents of Hartlepool United AFC. Of course, there are always dull academics who try to find some sort of 'hidden meaning'. Perhaps the loyal fishermen had actually hanged a real Frenchman, a young powder monkey. So-called because powder monkeys ran from magazine to cannon carrying cartridges of gunpowder during battle. A bit far-fetched? But no more than hanging uncommunicative primates.

Anyhow, whatever the origin, the term is now embraced with some pride. The local Rugby Union team are known as the Monkeyhangers. Hartlepool United AFC's mascot is H'Angus the Monkey. Incredibly in 2002 a joker called Stuart Drummond campaigned for the office of mayor in the costume of H'Angus the Monkey using the slogan 'free bananas for schoolchildren' and won. He went on to win a second term and turned out to be quite a worthwhile mayor. However, children never got free bananas.

'Make a Wish for the Monkey and give generously to the Alice House Hospice.' This version is perched precariously at the entrance to Hartlepool Marina.

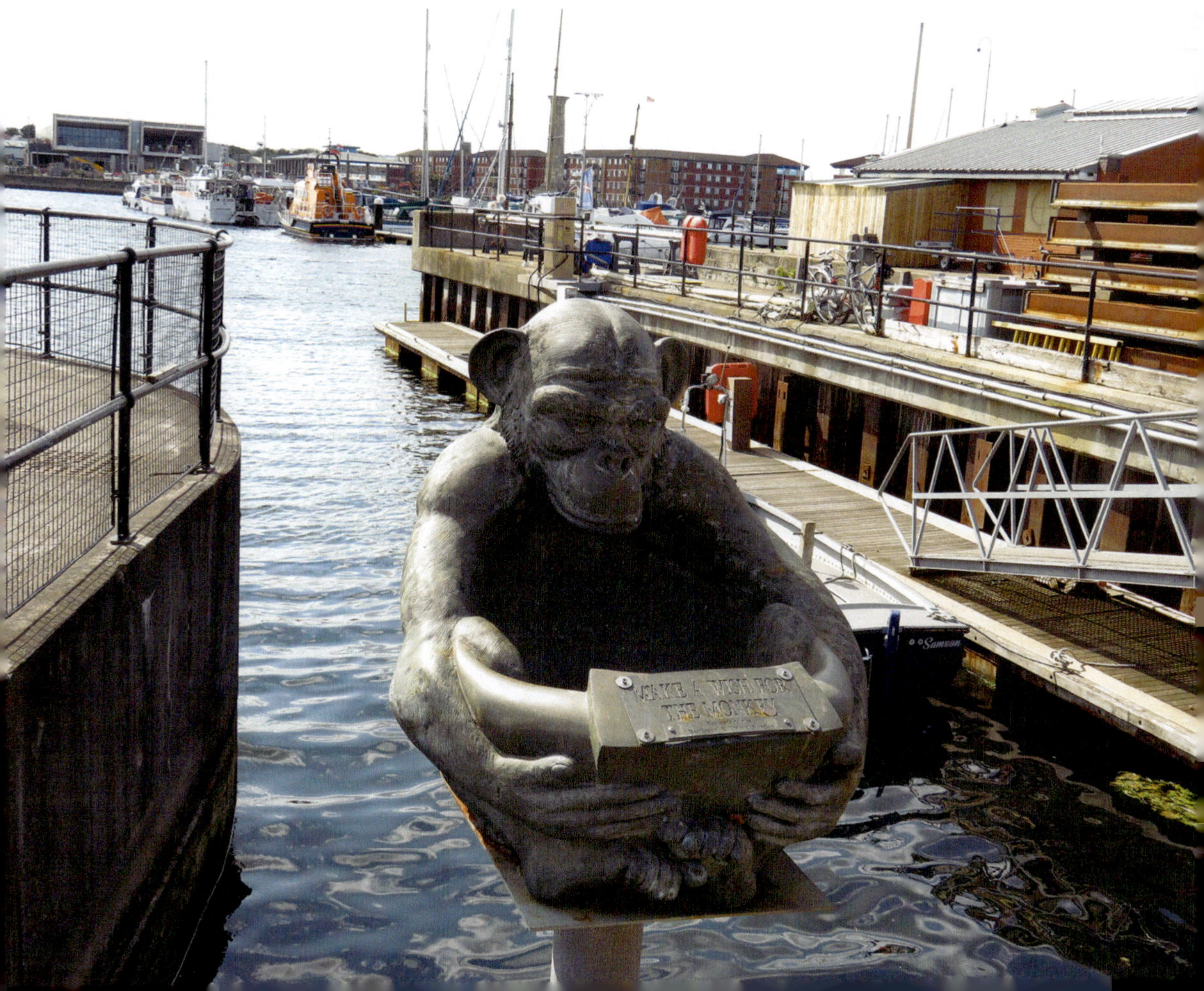

This strange story is not unique though. Boddam in North East Scotland is the possessor of a near-identical story set in 1772, and Greenock boasts an old ballad with the same theme. Mevagissy in Cornwall has the story of a child killed by a bite from an organ grinder's monkey for which it was tried and executed. Paul Screeton gives particular prominence to the song by Geordie comic singer Ned Corvan 'Who hung the monkey?' which first appeared in print in 1862. He suggests that Corvan adapted the Boddam song. Corvan was, apparently, in the habit of writing local ballads linked to various locations, which is one good way of guaranteeing sales.

Just north of Hartlepool, in Sunderland there was Spottee. He appeared from nowhere and took up residence in a sea cave. He could not converse with local people in their own language, so they believed him to be a shipwrecked foreigner or, even worse, a Frenchman. Some more sympathetic people believed Spottee was no more than a simple minded but harmless old tramp. In The *Bishoprick Garland* Sir Cuthbert Sharp describes him as such:

> He lived there for many years, wearing his spotty shirt, from which his name came. He earned his living by begging, doing odd jobs, and foraging along the beach. When his time came he died in his cave, and his ghost was to be seen for years afterwards out on stormy nights warning ships to stay away from the rocks as a saviour, or perhaps luring ships onto rocks as a wrecker! Local children, even in his lifetime, regarded him as a subject of all sorts of stories and to frighten each other and then after his death they saw his cave as a boggle hole.

Sadly, the killjoy Sunderland City Council keep Spottee's Cave locked up to avoid accidents. Oddly enough there is also a legend that there is a tunnel from it as far inland as Hylton Castle! When pushed, no one can explain why it should exist, if indeed it did, which it does not.

While I'm on the subject of Sunderland there is the question of the Black Cat. Sunderland AFC are known as 'the Black Cats'. There are two theories behind the nickname. The 'official' version is that in 1805 a coastal gun battery known as the John Paul Jones Battery was renamed the Black Cat Battery because a soldier called Josiah Dunn was returning to his post, no doubt suitably lubricated, when he heard an unearthly howling. He ran on believing the Devil to be following him. In fact, the 'Devil' was a black cat! Thus, the battery became known as the Black Cat Battery and this has been seen to be linked to the Josiah Dunn story. Another view is that a 4-1 home defeat to Liverpool on New Year's Day 1909 left Sunderland very near the bottom of the First Division but the next day when the players entered their changing room before a fixture against Bury they found a stray black cat had taken residence. Then there was no looking back and the team went from success to success with further League championships in 1913 and 1936, culminating in 1937 with their first FA Cup win.

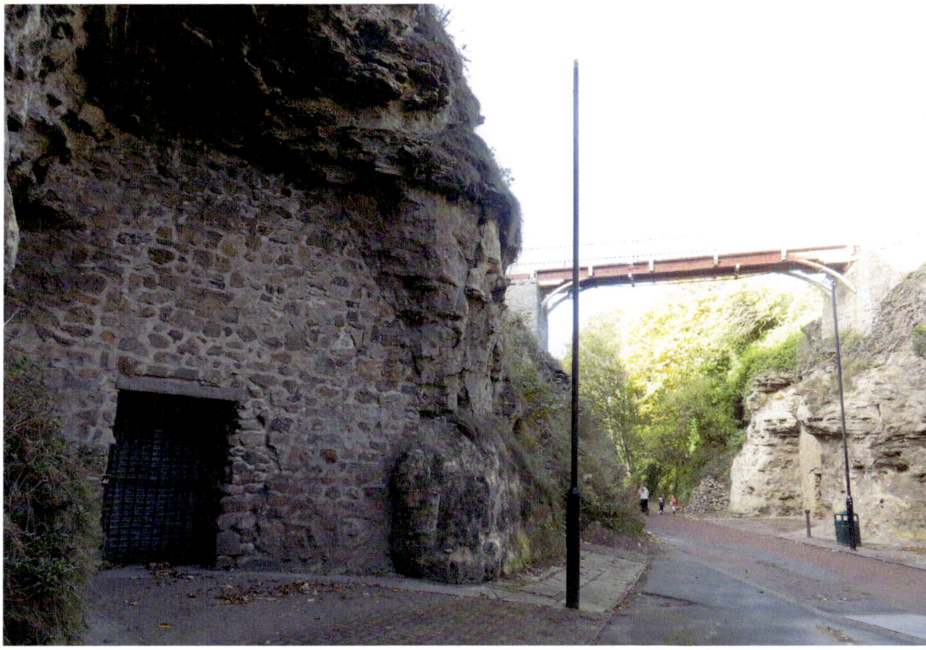

Spottee's Cave in Roker Park, near Roker Ravine. Supposedly a tunnel leads as far as Hylton Castle.

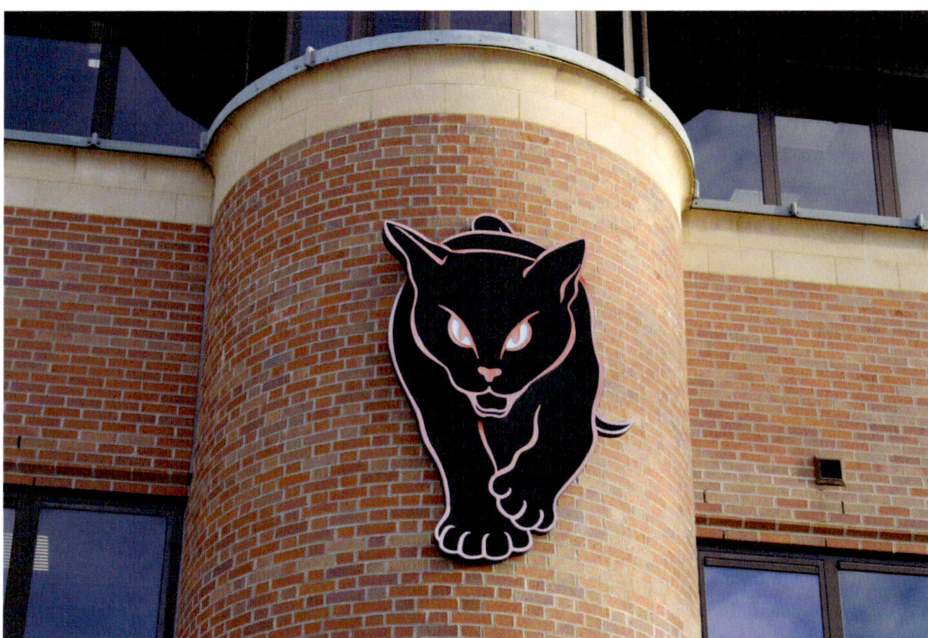

At Sunderland AFC's Stadium of Light black cats are everywhere: on the coat of arms, on football strips and creeping down walls as if to pounce on unwary Newcastle fans.

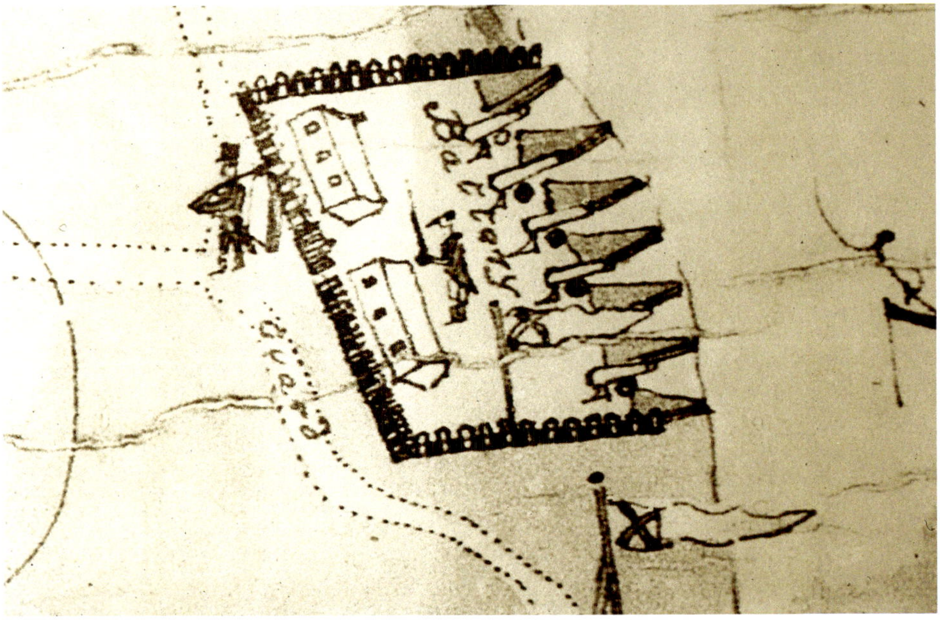

A gun battery shown on Rain's *Eye Plan* in *c.* 1785. One of the batteries was known as the 'John Paul Jones' or 'Black Cat Battery'. The *Eye Plan* is a remarkable contemporary depiction of life and activity in Sunderland in the thriving 1780s.

There is, though, an oddity about the Josiah Dunn story, and that is that it does not appear until about 2000 in connection with the Club. The story itself, whether true or not, does appear in the nineteenth century. I think one possibility is that it became popularised when it appeared in history books by the local publishing company called Black Cat, which also, coincidentally, published a Sunderland football annual at that time for several years.

The previous battery name arose from the American privateer John Paul Jones who was active in British waters during the War of Independence. Allegedly, he considered attacking the very combustible harbour of Sunderland but was scared off by crowds of what seemed to be British redcoats on the Town Moor. In fact, they were red shawl-clad women gathered to witness the approach of the charismatic buccaneer. The story has no basis in fact. However, something very similar did occur in February 1797 when a French force landed near Fishguard in Pembrokeshire and was defeated by local British forces. Their collapsing morale may have resulted partly from the appearance of crowds of aggressive local women dressed in red shawls and black steeple crowned hats.

Less of Sunderland, and now for the Devil and Staindrop. If you visit the delightful village you can see a stone face in the wall of a cottage staring into St Mary's churchyard. Over the road, jutting out of a wall is a stone limb, maybe a leg. I recall being told about this many years ago by an elderly gentleman whose version was that when the splendid 'Cathedral of the Dale' was about to

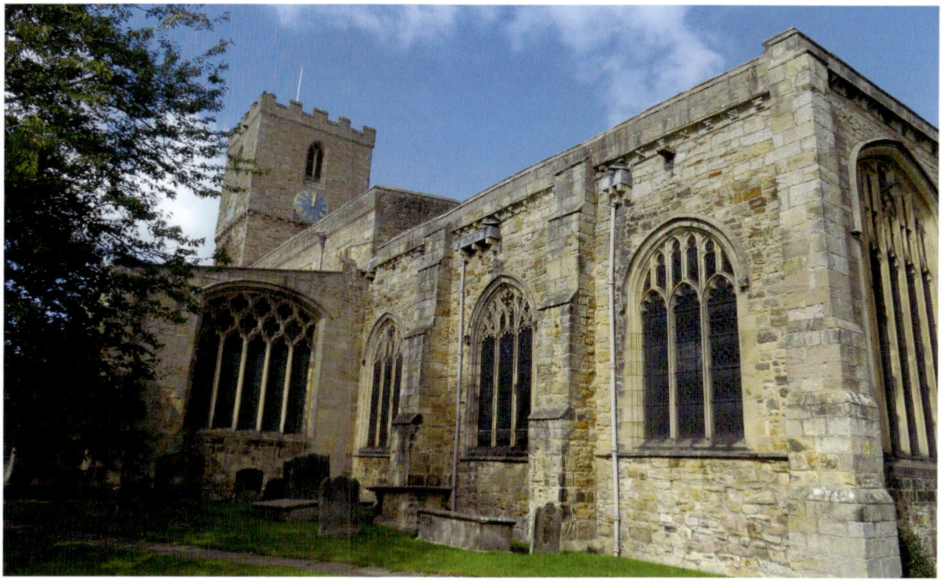

The Cathedral of the Dales is St Mary's in Staindrop, where the Devil, or more likely a Satanic imp, confronted St Michael and was flung from the top of the imposing tower.

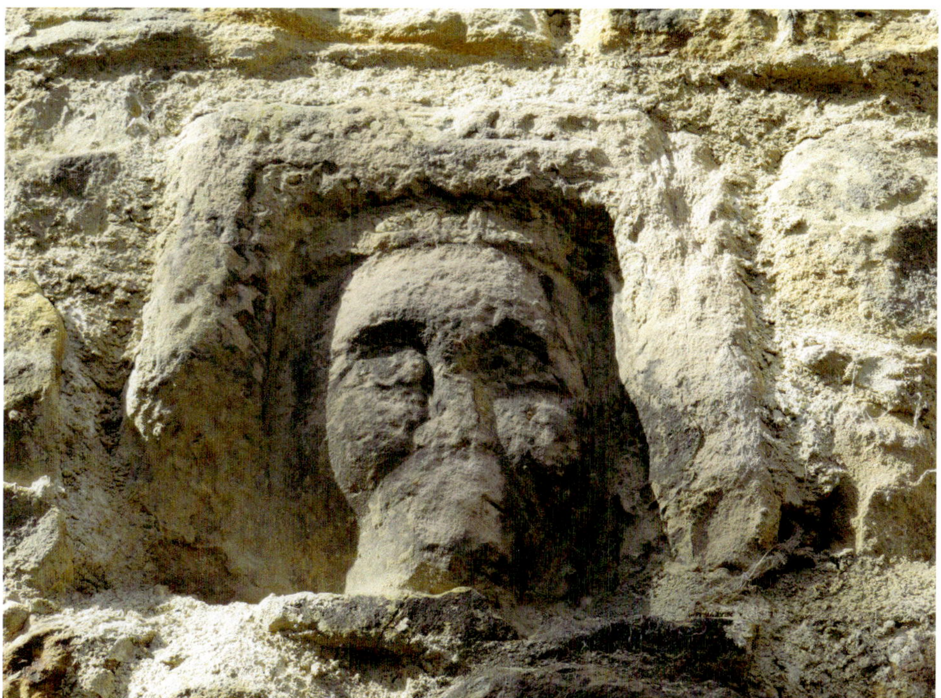

Is this the face of Satan you see before you? Or that of a devilish imp set in the wall of a cottage overlooking St Mary's churchyard in Staindrop?

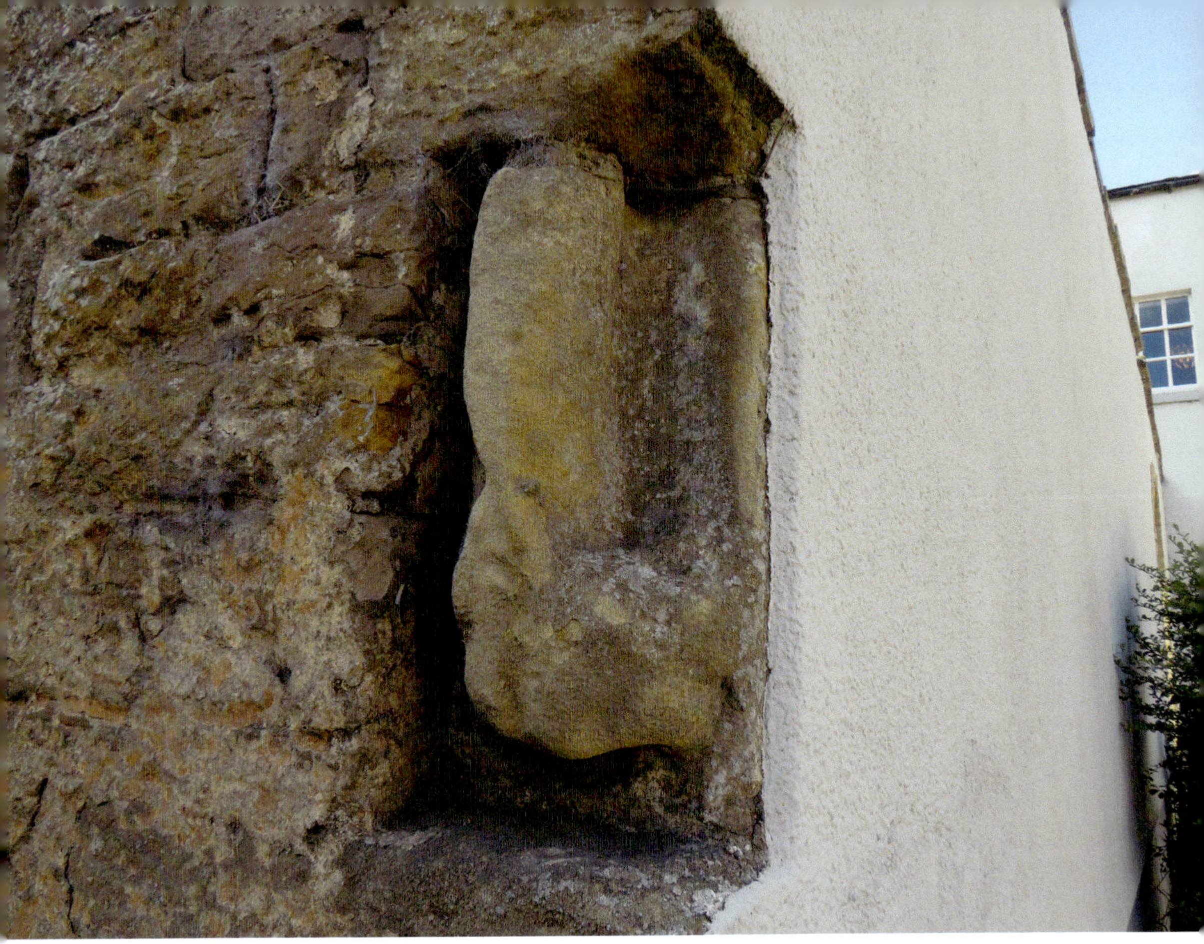

Perhaps a limb of the Devil himself, or at least one of his accomplices, set in stone in the main street of Staindrop. There may be other body parts yet to be discovered, I suppose.

be topped out, Satan materialised to prevent completion but was confronted by St Michael. Good triumphed in a bitter engagement, the Devil was cast down from the tower, and his body parts were scattered. If that was the case though this would surely undermine all religious faiths? The truth is that the features were taken from an early fifteenth-century college in the churchyard demolished in the 1480s.

Before Satan met this untimely death, he was very busy in Castle Eden Dene near the Durham Heritage Coast. If you follow the Yew Tree Trail you will encounter the Devil's Lapstone. It is said that he offered to help build Durham Cathedral intending to use crumbling rock so it would collapse. So he flew up and down merrily collecting stones. One day the leather pouch he was using to carry a massive boulder snapped. As it fell, he snatched at it leaving scratch marks on the surface. The Devil also promised to help a man called Gunner gather stone to build Durham Cathedral. Gunner was forbidden to look behind him as he led the way. Suddenly he heard a sound as if the sea was about to crash over him and turned around. The Devil was furious and hurled a huge rock at him. To this day poor Gunner lies beneath the rock beside a pool in a deep gorge named after him.

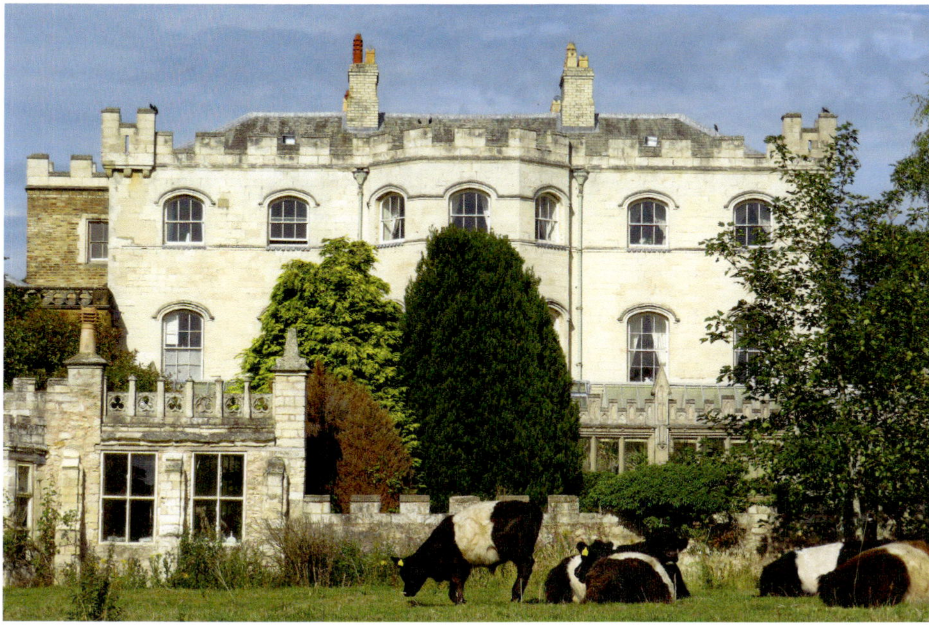

The eighteenth-century Palladian Castle at Castle Eden, one of the residences of the very wealthy Burdon family – bankers with a variety of related business interests. Most of the first-born men were called Rowland, which is a potential cause of confusion. Taken from the west from the roadside.

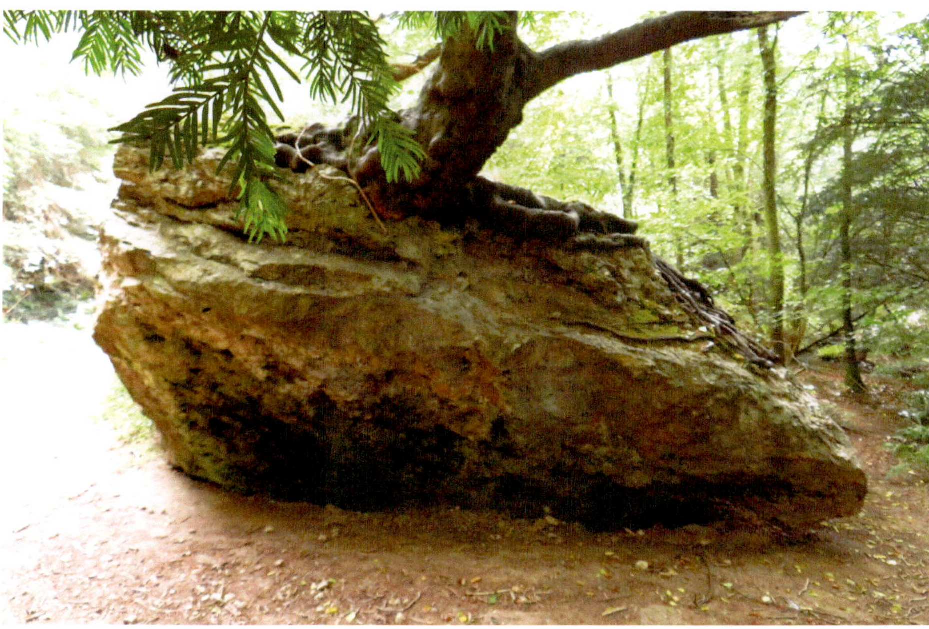

The Devil's Lapstone in Castle Eden Dene is a huge boulder with markings said to be scratches by the Devil.

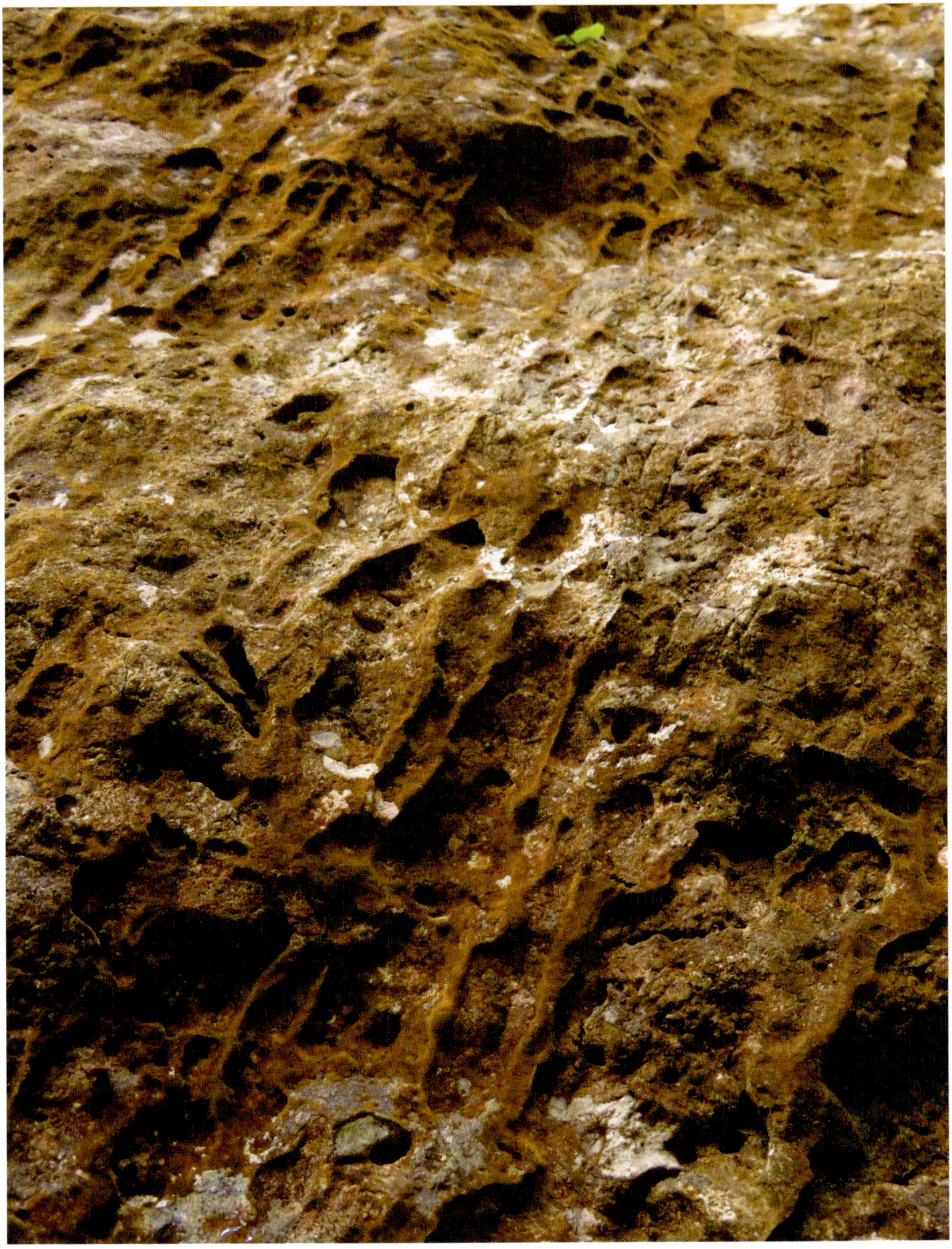

There is a curious latticework of markings on the south side of the boulder which, with a big stretch of the imagination, could be seen as scratches.

The Dene belonged in the eighteenth century to the very wealthy Burdon family. There is no evidence of the Satanic stories existing before it was laid out, but equally none that they were not. It is conceivable that they were created to add an air of Gothic mystique to the Dene for visitors. Or perhaps they were invented by adventurous Burdon children.

You don't get many giants in County Durham but there are the famous three brothers of the Derwent Valley. Cor, Ben and Con lived in caves in Corbridge in Northumberland and in Benfieldside and Consett in County Durham. Alarmingly, they fed on Christian flesh, and especially the delicate limbs of children. They uprooted pine trees to wield in fights and killed scores of men and women. They had a huge hammer which they could hurl for nine miles and passed it to each other in this way. In one case, Con mis-threw to his brother Cor and the result was a hole in the ground at Howden. Sometimes Cor is replaced by Mug who was the originator of the name Muggleswick. Thankfully they are no longer

A view over the Derwent near the Snape Wood and the unfindable cavern where King Arthur and his Knights of the Round Table await the call to awake and come to the aid of our threatened nation, solving our underlying economic growth and balance of payment problems.

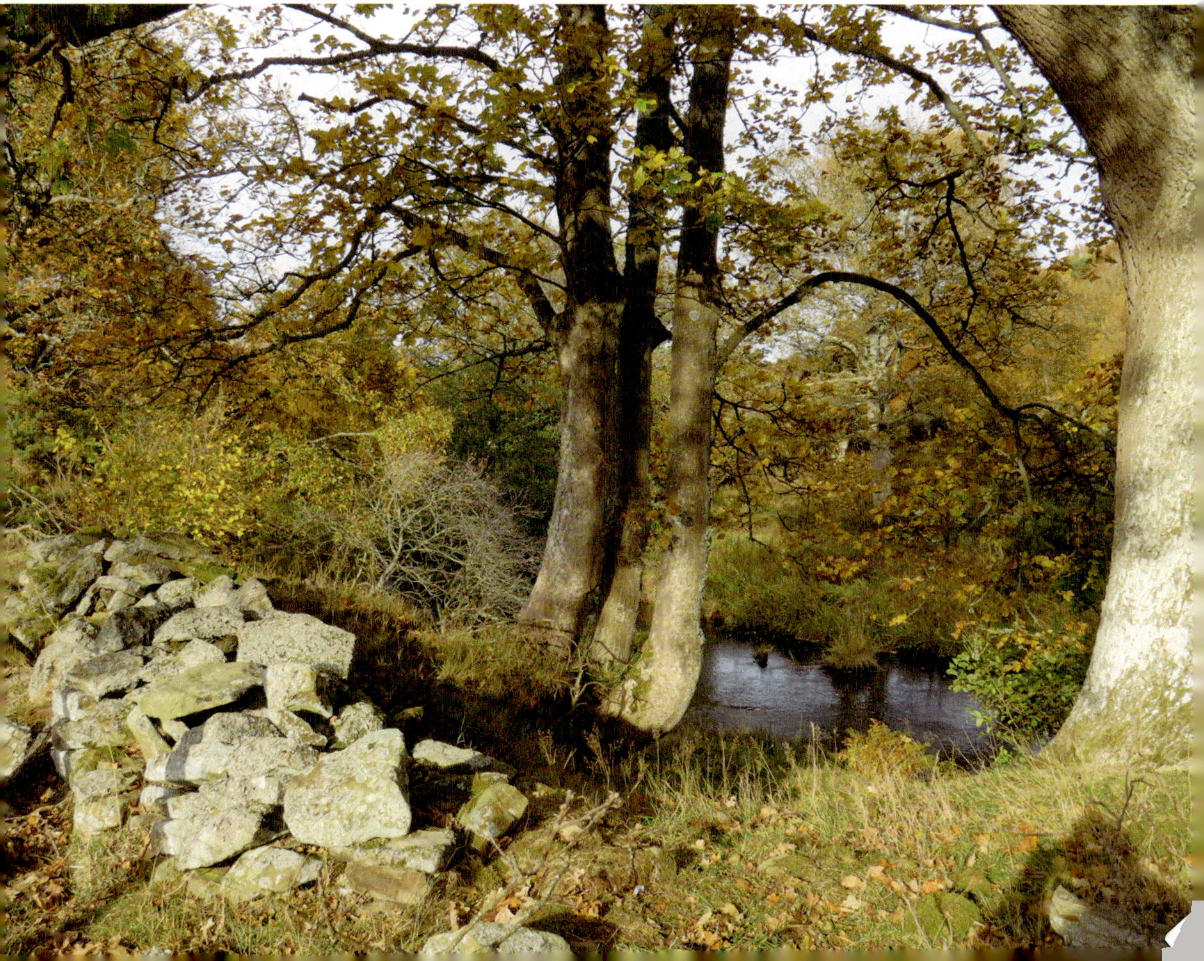

with us. Con was killed by an arrow at Annfield Plain, Ben died at the hands of Sir Lancelot at Medomsley and Mug was murdered with a spike in his head by a ravished nun. It takes all sorts.

Finally, where would we be without King Arthur and the Round Table? There is indeed at least one sighting in County Durham near Muggleswick. It is claimed that near the so-called Snape, a tongue of woodland within a horseshoe river bend, there is a cavern wherein King Arthur and his knights dwell, waiting for the call to rise and reclaim the kingdom. No one has ever found it. It's obviously one of those pop-up caverns which only materialises before the chosen one. I couldn't find it but all that means is that I'm not virtuous enough. Stories about hidden caverns and sleeping King Arthur are, frankly, ten-a-penny. One of the best is Guy the Seeker near Dunstanburgh where tourists get better value for money.

So, on that cynical note, we move to some sort of conclusion.

Conclusion: Back to the Future

That's the end of my selection. It's comprehensive but by no means exhaustive. There is no such thing as an 'Age of Folk Tales' because that would imply some sort of end point. Folk tales are constantly dying and disappearing as chains of transmission are broken. Those which exist today will be only a fraction of the total. However, they are still being generated. Social media is now serving the same process of transmission and development, albeit with unimaginable speed and accessibility.

Conspiracy theories have very much in common with folk tales. They seek to explain events through hidden forces. They offer a sense of order when the 'official' explanations are inadequate. They exhibit an evolving collective narrative. They help to reinforce group identity and appeal to such emotions as fear and suspicion. On the other hand, conspiracy theories thrive on division, and possession of 'the knowledge' which excludes non-believers while folk tales tend to have a unifying influence at a regional or national level.

Finally, there is a word that I've avoided but which is vital to the understanding of the creation of folk tales and conspiracy theories and that is 'gullibility' – the inability to separate fact from fiction and to think critically. Although we now live in an age of mass state education that very modern version of folk tales, conspiracy theories, thrives where plausibility meets gullibility.

Bibliography

Hallowell, Michael J., *The House that Jack Built: The True Story Behind the Marsden Grotto and the Search for Roman Treasure* (Amberley, 2008)

Grice, Frederick, *Folk Tales of the North Country* (Thomas Nelson & Sons Ltd, 1944)

Appleton, Arthur, *The Mystery of the Duke of Perth: A Historical Enigma* (2002)

Brockie, William, *Legends and Superstitions of the County of Durham* (Sunderland. B. Williams, 1886)

Surtees, Robert, *The History and Antiquities of the County Palatine of Durham* (London Nichols, Son, and Bentley, Sunderland, 1816–1840; Hills, 1908)

Hayward, Arthur, Lawrence, *Lives of the Most Remarkable Criminals Who have been Condemned and Executed for Murder, the Highway, Housebreaking, Street Robberies, Coining or Other Offences* (1874) Sykes, John, *Local Records: Historical Register of remarkable events, which have occurred in Northumberland and Durham, Newcastle upon Tyne, and Berwick upon Tweed*, 1833

Henderson, William *Notes on the folk-lore of the northern countries of England and the borders* (1879)

Greenwell, Bill, *Marsden Rock and Marsden Grotto* (Sunnyside Press, 2020)

Screeton, Paul, *Who Hung the Monkey?: Story of the Hartlepool Legend* (1991)

Fivecoate, Jesse A. and Kitta, Andrea (eds.), *Whispers in the Echo Chamber: Folklore and the Role of Conspiracy Theory in Contemporary Society* (University of Wisconsin Press, 2025)

Scully, Val, *Tales of Derwentdale and the extraordinary J. W. Fawcett* (first published in 1902. A second edition was published in 2019 by Land of Oak and Iron with the addition of the biography of J. W. Fawcett)

Lawrence, Natalie, *Enchanted Creatures: Our Monsters and Their Meanings* (Weidenfeld and Nicolson, 2024)

Leighton, Henry R. (ed.), *Memorials of Old Durham* (George Allen and Sons, 1910)

Rollason, David (ed.), *Libellus de exordio atque procurso istius, hoc est Dunhelmensis Tract on the Origins and Progress of the Church of Durham* by Symeon of Durham (OUP, 2000)

Jacobs, Joseph, *English Fairy Tales* (David Nutt, 1890)

Jacobs, Joseph, *More English Fairy Tales* (David Nutt, 1894)

Whitlock, Ralph, *Here Be Dragons* (George Allen and Unwin, 1983)

Summers, Jeremiah William, *The History and Antiquities of Sunderland, Bishopwearmouth, Bishopwearmouth Panns, Burdon, Ford, Ryhope, Silksworth, Tunstall, Monkwearmouth, Monkwearmouth Shore, Fulwell, Hylton and Southwick* (Joseph Tate, 1858)

Burney, William (ed.), *Tales and Traditions of Teesdale* (Teesdale Mercury, 1885)

Hartland, Edwin Sidney (ed.), *English Fairy and other Folk Tales*

Howitt, William, *The Rural Life of England*, second edition (Longman, Orme, Brown, Green and Longmans, 1840)

Philip, Neil, *The Penguin Book of English Folktales* (Penguin, 1992. Reprinted by Watkins, 2022)

Schneidau, Lisa, *Woodland Folk Tales of Britain and Ireland* (History Press, 2020)

Schneidau, Lisa, *Botanical Folk Tales of Britain and Ireland* (History Press, 2018)

Chainey, Dee Dee, *A Treasury of British Folklore* (National Trust, 2024)

Strang, Veronica, *Water Beings: From Nature Worship to Environmental Crisis* (Reaktion Books, 2023)

Gregson, Keith, *Corvan: A Victorian Entertainer and His Songs* (Oxford, Kemble, 1983)

Lomas, Richard, *An Encyclopaedia of North-East England* (Edinburgh, Birlinn, 2009)

Acknowledgements

My thanks are due to the following people: Marie Gardiner of Lonely Tower for establishing contact with Amberley Publishing for me in the first place, and in general for the good friendship of herself and Mark. Nick Grant of Amberley Publishing for his help with the original commissioning, and for being available for consultation and advice throughout. Ron Stout, formerly of the *Sunderland Echo*, who proofread for me, politely discouraged my much more imaginative use of commas and warned me against entering the minefield of whether the Venerable Bede was a Jarrow or Monkwearmouth man. William Jones for his help with some of the illustrations, and especially with Bosely the Boar. Rosie Callaghan for her availability to help with illustrations which will be taken up for a future project. Edward Scott of Middridge Grange Farm who spent a good while discussing the Middridge Fairies with me and the restoration of the lovely medieval farmhouse. Mrs Winter and her daughters of Crooked Oak Farm who let me take photographs of their home and advised me about the fearsome witch Jane Frizzle and her supposed burial place. Rob Mason, the historian of Sunderland AFC, for his help with the strange story of the origin of the Black Cat nickname and emblem of Sunderland AFC. Various members of the congregations of St Andrew's Church in Bishop Auckland and St Margaret of Antioch's Church in Durham for their help with Richard Pollard the brawn-killer and Sir John Duck, respectively.